Collins Colour Guides
BIRDS
Swifts to Finches

COLLINS COLOUR GUIDES

BIRDS
Swifts to Finches

CLAUS KÖNIG

Translated from the German by
H. MAYER-GROSS

Illustrated with 136 colour photographs

COLLINS
St. James's Place, London

Cover photograph: Golden Oriole
Frontispiece: Great Spotted Woodpecker

ISBN 0 00 212038-0
First published in German by Chr. Belser Verlag, Stuttgart,
under the title EUROPÄISCHE VÖGEL I, in 1966.

CONTENTS

Foreword 8
Introduction 10
Swifts (Apodidae) 18
Nightjars (Caprimulgidae) 22
Kingfishers (Alcedinidae) 23
Bee-eaters (Meropidae) 26
Rollers (Coraciidae) 30
Hoopoes (Upupidae) 31
Woodpeckers (Picidae) 34
Larks (Alaudidae) 47
Swallows (Hirundinidae) 55
Orioles (Oriolidae) 59
Crows (Corvidae) 62
Tits (Paridae) 83
Penduline Tits (Remizidae) 95
Long-tailed Tits (Aegithalidae) 98
Babblers (Timaliidae) 99
Nuthatches (Sittidae) 102
Treecreepers (Certhiidae) 106
Wrens (Troglodytidae) 107
Dippers (Cinclidae) 110
Thrushes, Warblers, Flycatchers, etc.
(Muscicapidae) 111
Accentors (Prunellidae) 182
Pipits and Wagtails (Motacillidae) 183
Waxwings (Bombycillidae) 191
Shrikes (Laniidae) 194
Starlings (Sturnidae) 199
Finches (Fringillidae) 202
Weavers (Ploceidae) 239
Topography of a bird and identification features 245
Practical bird conservation 247
Explanation of scientific names 249
Abbreviations of authors' names 252
Index 253
List of photographers 256

FOREWORD

There are a great many books on birds, but very few in which they are illustrated entirely by colour photographs. This is understandable, since it is extremely difficult to bring together good colour reproductions of all the species which a book following a systematic list must cover. Nevertheless it has proved possible to illustrate here nearly all the important European members of the "near-Passerine" Orders—nightjars, swifts, rollers and woodpeckers—and of the Passerines or perching birds. Anyone who has ever tried his hand at bird photography will know how much patience is required to obtain just *one* good picture, without upsetting the bird in the process. The publishers and I wish to thank all the photographers concerned for their generous assistance.

The short review on the following pages introduces each Order of birds and mentions the features which closely related families have in common. In the main part of the book the chief identification-features—voice, distribution, the surroundings usually favoured (habitat), breeding biology and food—are described for each illustrated species. As the birds were photographed from various distances, their true size cannot be gauged from the plates; however, actual measurements are given in the text. My grateful thanks are due to Prof. Dr. E. Schüz and Dr. H. Löhrl for their critical reading of the manuscript and helpful suggestions. A second volume covers the remaining Orders of birds represented in Europe, and briefly reviews the most important literature.

Claus König

INTRODUCTION

The classification of the bird world dates back, like that of the whole of the animal and plant world, to the 10th edition of the "Systema Naturae" produced by Carl von Linné (Carolus Linnaeus) in 1758. 554 species of birds were described in it.

Among the vertebrates birds constitute, next to the fishes, the class with the greatest number of species. Whereas at present about 18,000 kinds of fish are known, the class "Aves" (birds) contains roughly 8,500 species. These are divided into 28 different orders, of which the order "Passeriformes" (perching birds) is the largest, with over 5,000 species.

The branch of science which concerns itself with the classification of creatures according to their relationship and ancestry in the "natural system" is called "systematics" or "taxonomy". The classification of a bird used nowadays may be demonstrated with the Great Grey Shrike *(Lanius excubitor)*:

Kingdom: Animals (Animalia)
Phylum: Vertebrates (Vertebrata)
Class: Birds (Aves)
Order: Perching birds (Passeriformes)
Family: Shrikes (Laniidae)
Genus: Shrikes *(Lanius)*
Species: Great Grey Shrike *(L. excubitor)*
Subspecies: Spanish Great Grey Shrike (*L. e. meridionalis* Linnaeus 1758)

The scientific name of a bird is formed of the generic and specific name (binomial nomenclature). If a special race or "subspecies" is to be named, the subspecific designation is added (trinomial nomenclature). The name and year often placed after the scientific name indicates the name of the person who first described this form and the date the description was published. The author's name is usually abbreviated, and in many cases both it and the year are omitted.

The class "Aves" contains 28 orders:

1. Sphenisciformes (Penguins)
2. Struthioniformes (Ostriches)
3. Casuariiformes (Cassowaries)
4. Apterygiformes (Kiwis)
5. Rheiformes (Rheas)
6. Tinamiformes (Tinamous)
7. *Gaviiformes* (Divers)
8. *Podicipediformes* (Grebes)
9. *Procellariiformes* (Petrels and Albatrosses)
10. *Pelecaniformes* (Pelicans, Cormorants, Boobies, Frigate-birds)
11. *Ciconiiformes* (Herons, Storks)
12. *Phoenicopteriformes* (Flamingos)
13. *Anseriformes* (Ducks, Geese and Swans)
14. *Falconiformes* (Hawks and Vultures)
15. *Galliformes* (Game-birds)
16. *Gruiformes* (Cranes, Rails, Bustards)
17. *Charadriiformes* (Waders, Gulls and Auks)
18. *Columbiformes* (Doves, Sandgrouse)
19. Psittaciformes (Parrots and Cockatoos)
20. *Cuculiformes* (Cuckoos, Turacos)
21. *Strigiformes* (Owls)
22. *Caprimulgiformes* (Nightjars)
23. *Apodiformes* (Swifts, Hummingbirds)
24. Coliiformes (Mousebirds)
25. Trogoniformes (Trogons)
26. *Coraciiformes* (Rollers, Hoopoes, Bee-eaters, Kingfishers)
27. *Piciformes* (Woodpeckers, Toucans, Barbets, Honey-guides)
28. *Passeriformes* (Passerine or perching birds)

The orders shown in italics are those which have representatives in Europe, comprising a total of about 460 species.

Approximately 430 of these are breeding species, while the rest touch Europe (especially the coastal regions) more or less regularly as migrants. To these must be added some 120 so-called "vagrants" which only occasionally stray into Europe. In many cases the species which breed in Europe do not stay put after the breeding season, but undertake movements, which may be very long. These are the summer visitors or—as they have often been termed—the migrants. Bird migration still holds many riddles for us; many ornithological stations and institutes are engaged in its study. For this an important technique is scientific ringing, in which the birds have a numbered aluminium ring placed round one leg, giving the address of the ringing organisation or station. With many kinds of bird it has been possible by this means to find out the routes they follow and where they spend the winter. The way in which migrating birds orientate themselves is still the subject of much research. From the results obtained so far, we can say that the species which move by day find their direction chiefly from the sun and from specific landmarks. At night the stars appear to play an important role in orientation, and, under very cloudy conditions, possibly even the earth's magnetic field—though this last is by no means generally accepted. Birds travelling at night—particularly if it is foggy—are attracted to bright sources of light such as lit-up cities or lighthouses.

European birds may be divided into three broad groups:

1. *Residents* are those which stay the whole year in their breeding area and do not move about much.
2. *Partial migrants* are species which after breeding move in a predominantly southerly direction, mainly stopping to winter in mid- or western Europe or in the Mediterranean countries. The so-called "winter visitors" may be included among these partial migrants.
3. *Summer visitors* are only found in Europe during the warmer months of the year. They spend the winter for the most part in tropical Africa.

It was formerly customary to distinguish between 1. residents, 2. passage-migrants, 3. winter and summer visitors.

Brief survey of the orders in this volume

Swifts (Apodiformes)

This order contains two families: the swifts which are represented in Europe by three species of the genus *Apus*, and the hummingbirds (Trochilidae) whose distribution is confined to America. The swifts resemble swallows in having long sickle-like wings. The legs are very short, with feet specially adapted for clinging, since all four toes are directed forwards and are equipped with strong claws.

These birds spend most of their lives in flight; at night parties of Swifts have been observed actually "dozing" over towns, making use of warm rising air (thermals). These species generally tend to roost in crannies in walls, rock-crevices and tree-holes. In outbreaks of bad weather they can often survive for some days without food, as long as the periods do not last too long. They also frequently make long "weather-evading" flights. They build their nests in holes and clefts with material collected in the air, cemented with saliva. Some species—among them the Alpine Swift *(Apus melba)*—often glue their nests like cups to vertical surfaces inside a hole. The young feed by snatching at the adult's beak and grasping its head as far as the forehead within their gape. This causes it to regurgitate and transfer the food.

Young Swifts sometimes climb out of their nests before they are fully grown and fall to the ground. The parents will not feed them on the ground, so if you come upon any you should if possible put them back in the nest. The young can also be hand-reared—though this needs patience. Whey mixed up with ant pupae (fresh or dried), is made into pea-sized pellets which are gently pushed down the young Swift's throat. These can be alternated with small amounts of minced meat, squashed mealworms, flies, etc. Since young Swifts do not "gape", i. e. raise and open their beaks, one must carefully open their beaks and push the food in with blunt forceps. Feeding must be kept up until the flight feathers are fully grown and their bases no longer enclosed by waxy quill sheaths. Then one only has to toss the Swifts gently into the air, and off they fly. They do not have to be taught how to catch their food—the ability is innate. When rearing them special care should be taken that the birds do not soil themselves and that they get sufficient nourishment, which means two to three pellets every hour right through the day.

Nightjars or Goatsuckers (Caprimulgiformes)

The nightjars, also known as goatsuckers or nighthawks, form an order containing 5 families, of which only one, the true nightjars (Caprimulgidae), occurs in Europe, two species of one genus being found. This group consists predominantly of woodland species, but some inhabit semi-desert regions. They are characterised by soft plumage patterned like bark, and by an extremely wide gape. The flight silhouette is somewhat falcon-like.

The name "goatsucker" apparently originated in the fact that ignorant countryfolk, coming across these birds near their farmyards or goatsheds in the daytime, believed that they used their enormous gape to suck milk from their goats' teats. Because of their nocturnal habits, many superstitious people considered them—like owls—to be evil.

Both European species breed on the ground and, thanks to the protective colouration of their plumage, are extremely hard to see. No nests whatever are built, but eggs are laid directly on to the ground. When they hatch the young are already covered with greyish-brown down and after only a few days can run a short distance from the nest site. When it is fed the youngster grasps the adult's beak completely within its gape while food is regurgitated.

The birds roost during the day, preferring to perch lengthwise on thicker branches, with their large eyes closed to a narrow slit.

Rollers (Coraciiformes)

This group contains 7 families. Four of these are represented in Europe, each by one species: the true rollers (Coraciidae), kingfishers (Alcedinidae), bee-eaters (Meropidae) and hoopoes (Upupidae).

When they are half-grown, nestling rollers, bee-eaters and kingfishers look "prickly" because all their feathers are still completely enclosed in the quill sheaths. They do not open out until about a week before fledging. In this way serious soiling of the feathers is largely prevented in these somewhat unhygienic birds. When feeding, parents gently touch the base of the bill of the young with a morsel and they snatch at it. Later on the adults simply hold food in front of their young, who unceremoniously grab it from them. Only one chick gets fed at each visit. With kingfishers especially there is a characteristic "feeding-merry-go-round": the replete nestling backs away from the mouth to the side of the nest-chamber and the next one slips into its place. In this way the food gets evenly allocated.

Young Hoopoes "gape" like passerines when their parents arrive with food, which is then stuffed down one of the widely-opened beaks. Hoopoe chicks also have yellowish-white gape-flanges much like those of young passerines. Hoopoes' nest-holes are no dirtier than those of other hole-breeders. The assertion that they are like cesspools arises from the fact that if apparent danger threatens the young squirt a stinking secretion from their uropygial glands in order to scare off the attacker. This foul-smelling stuff is no longer formed by the young once they have flown. The nestlings' faeces are excreted as encapsulated pellets, and the parents keep the nest-hole clean by removing these.

Woodpeckers (Piciformes)

The woodpecker order is composed of 6 families: puffbirds (Bucconidae), jacamars (Galbulidae), barbets (Capitonidae), true woodpeckers (Picidae), toucans (Ramphastidae) and honeyguides (Indicatoridae). Of these only one family, the Picidae with ten species, occurs in Europe. Except for the Wryneck *(Jynx torquilla)* all these birds excavate their own nest-hole in trunks and boughs of trees. None uses any nest material. In the course of feeding the young grasp the bill of the parent, which then regurgitates food from its crop. Even in their nest-holes woodpeckers are unsociable and often quarrel with each other. Many species use a mechanically produced drumming instead of a song, but some have a series of ringing calls.

Perching birds (Passeriformes)

Over 5,000 species belong to this order—over half the total species known in the world. They are divided into more than 50 families, which are spread over the whole world and can be found in every habitat. The largest sub-order consists of the "song birds" (Oscines); all the forms occurring in Europe belong to this sub-order. The biggest of these is the Raven *(Corvus corax)*, weighing fully 2 lb, while the smallest is the Goldcrest *(Regulus regulus)*, under $1/5$ oz in weight.

When they hatch nestling passerines are blind and often completely naked or have a little down on the upperparts, and they all have one characteristic in common: they "gape". In "gaping" heads are stretched upwards and the beaks opened wide. The insides of the mouths of young passerines are in most cases brightly coloured and sometimes patterned. At the base of both mandibles they also have more or less strikingly coloured "flanges".

Many kinds, especially open-nesting ones, tend to leave the nest even before they can fly, and hide among the vegetation. They have special calls to attract the attention of their parents which can then easily find and feed them. If one sees a fledgling which is unable to fly fluttering about among the bushes or on the ground it is quite wrong to assume that it has been abandoned by its parents. Such youngsters should be left alone, or, if found on a track or road where there are many people or cars, they should be gently placed in the nearest bush or on a safe twig. Since birds have a weak sense of smell, the parents do not notice when their young have been handled. However young House Martins *(Delichon urbica)* which have fallen from the nest do not get fed on the ground by their parents, so they should be replaced in the nest, or if this is impossible, hand-reared like young Swifts, and, once they are able to fly really well, released near a House Martin gathering.

◁ **Alpine Swift** · *Apus melba* (L.)

Family: Swifts (Apodidae)
Description: Both sexes are grey-brown above with a slight metallic sheen. The underside is pure white except for the grey-brown breast-band. Young birds may be recognised by the pale edges to their feathers. L: 8¹/₄", Wt: 3¹/₂ oz.

Especially in the morning and evening Alpine Swifts fly in parties round their breeding places, uttering loud series of trills which are very characteristic of this species. Single "hee" call notes may be heard too.

Distribution: Mediterranean countries, northwards to Switzerland and in Freiburg in south Germany (where it may be spreading), eastwards to India and the Himalayas; it also occurs in south and east Africa. The Alpine Swift is very rare in Britain, only a few birds which have wandered off-course being seen each year between spring and autumn. The species is a summer visitor which winters in tropical and southern Africa. It always arrives at the breeding quarters several weeks earlier than the Swift, and also migrates south later.
Habitat: Steep-sided ravines and high old buildings. When feeding it often travels long distances from its breeding sites.

Breeding: The nesting sites are similar to those used by Swifts. The two species also resemble each other in habits and behaviour. The actual nests are very like Swifts', but bigger. The clutch consists most often of three pure white eggs; incubation is shared by both sexes and lasts about 20 days. The young fly when they are just short of two months old, but often leave the nest earlier and clamber about nearby. Only one brood a year is reared.
Food: Flying insects of all kinds.

Swift · *Apus apus* (L.) ▷

Family: Swifts (Apodidae)

Description: The plumage of both sexes is—apart from the pale, sometimes near-white throat—smoky-black with patches of metallic sheen. The wings are long and crescent-like, the tail short and forked. All four toes are turned forwards and have strong claws. Juveniles resemble the parents, although the pale patch on the throat is larger and the feathers have pale edgings. The ♀♀ are generally a bit lighter in weight. L: *c.* 6½″, Wt: 1²/₅ oz.

Swifts are social birds which often indulge in dashing flights round chimneys, towers and eaves of houses, uttering their familiar shrill screaming call notes.

Distribution: The whole of Europe except the extreme north, north Africa and large stretches of Asia. The Swift occurs almost everywhere in mainland Britain and Ireland, and breeds on some islands. It is a summer visitor, wintering in tropical and southern Africa.

Habitat: It breeds in towns and villages, ruins and (in some countries) at times in cliffs and open woods with hollow trees.

Breeding: Crannies in walls, rock-crevices, cavities under tiles and eaves, special nestboxes and sometimes tree-holes serve as nest sites. Once a site is chosen, the birds often return faithfully to it. The nest is a shallow saucer of straws, feathers and leaves collected by the birds in flight. The material is coated with saliva which holds the whole structure together when it is dry. The two or three pure white elongated eggs are incubated by both partners, the incubation period being on average 20 days. The young stay in or close to the nest for some 42 days. This species has only one brood a year.

Food: Flying and wind-blown insects.

Allied Species:

The Pallid Swift (*Apus pallidus*), a very similar species to the Swift, inhabits the Mediterranean area and north Africa. It is browner in colour and its very pale throat-patch is larger. The Pallid Swift's voice is deeper than the Swift's. It breeds for preference in fissures in the entrances of large caves, especially on the sea-coast.

◁ **Nightjar** (Goatsucker) · *Caprimulgus europaeus* L. Above

Family: Nightjars (Caprimulgidae)
Description: Both sexes are greyish-brown in plumage with "scaly bark" patterning. In addition the ♂ has white marks on the primaries and at the tips of the outer tail feathers. The buoyant, twisting flight is very characteristic. L: *c.* 10¹/₂″, Wt: *c.* 2²/₃ oz.

The song consists of a continuous churring, which keeps varying in pitch; it sounds from a distance like the engine of a motor-cycle. At times ♂ and ♀ give fairly loud nasal calls like "coo-ic"; a high-pitched "ticking" is used when excited.

Distribution: The Nightjar breeds over almost all of Europe and large parts of Asia, and is also to be met with in north Africa. It is a summer visitor, wintering in east and south Africa.
Habitat: Heathland with scattered trees, open woods with rides and clearings, young forestry plantations.

Breeding: In display the ♂ claps loudly with its wings and shows its white "flashes". The nesting site is always on the ground and very frequently is completely unsheltered. No nest is built. The clutch almost always consists of two eggs, which are spotted and clouded with greyish-brown on a whitish ground. Both partners share the work of incubation, although it is chiefly the ♀ which broods. Incubation takes barely three weeks and after about another three weeks the young are capable of flight. Two broods are usually produced in a year.
Food: Entirely insects, especially moths. The bird mostly catches its prey during flight, but also picks it off the ground, while moving at a clumsy run.

Allied species:
The similar Red-necked Nightjar *(Caprimulgus ruficollis)* also occurs in southern Spain, Portugal, North Africa. Its song resembles a rhythmical knocking on a hollow branch.

◁ **Kingfisher** · *Alcedo atthis*. Nest-chamber

Kingfisher · *Alcedo atthis* (L.) ▷

Family: Kingfishers (Alcedinidae)
Description: The upperparts are brilliant bluish-green or turquoise, the throat is yellowish-white, underside brownish-red; the bird's legs are short and red. Its bill is long and pointed, the tail very short. Both sexes are similar in colouring, while the juveniles are somewhat paler with larger throat-patch and shorter bill. L: 6¹/₄″, Wt: 1¹/₄ oz.

The only call usually heard is a piercing whistle, which may be rendered as "cheet"; during the display period the ♂ makes a shrill short trill.

Distribution: Almost all Europe, north Africa, large parts of Asia down to Indonesia, but nowhere abundant. It is a resident, which outside the breeding season only scatters locally. In winter some birds move to the coast.
Habitat: The Kingfisher needs reasonably clean water. For preference it lives by streams and ponds with bushes or trees fringing the banks.

Breeding: Sandy or clay banks of rivers and pools, usually steep but sometimes more sloping—occasionally also banks some distance from water—serve as breeding sites. Kingfishers are solitary outside the breeding season. Pair formation, during which the partners noisily chase each other, occurs in early spring. Both birds dig a tunnel some 2 ins wide and up to 4 ft long, which slopes slightly upwards and opens out like an oven at the end. A nest is not constructed. The ♀ lays on average seven white roundish eggs on the floor of the nest-chamber, which gradually gets lined by ejected fishbone pellets. Both partners participate in incubation, although the ♂ occasionally feeds the ♀. The young, completely naked at first, hatch after about three weeks' incubation. They gradually develop quills, but these only open out about a week before fledging, so for a long time the chicks look "spiky". No attempt is made to remove their rather fluid excrement, which is squirted down the tunnel and may even flow out of the entrance hole. After barely four weeks the young Kingfishers fly out and scatter after only a few days. The parents often breed a second time, after which the partners separate and wander on their own.

Food: The Kingfisher preys on small water creatures, mainly fish, rarely more than 3 ins long, but also on small crustaceans and larvae of water insects. It usually chooses familiar lookout places and often sits motionless for minutes on end on an overhanging twig or on a post sticking out of the water. It catches its prey by diving, and then beats it thoroughly against a perch before swallowing it head-first.

Remarks: The Kingfisher has greatly decreased in many regions. Increasing pollution of waterways, elimination of natural banks and (in some countries) persecution by fish-breeders are among the prime causes of this decline. Severe winters can also have a very damaging effect on the population. For example the cold winter of 1962—63 killed off a high proportion of the population in Britain. The maintenance of unpolluted river-systems with natural banks is the key to the preservation of this jewel of the bird world.

Bee-eater · *Merops apiaster* L. (Illustration follows p. 27)

Family: Bee-eaters (Meropidae)
Description: The head and nape are chestnut-brown, the back golden-brown. Many individuals, especially ♀♀, have a greenish tinge over the rump. The flight feathers are bluish-green, as also is the tail with its two pointed centre feathers projecting markedly. The underparts are turquoise-blue with a bright yellow throat. The iris is ruby-red. Young birds are paler, with only a hint of projecting central tail feathers, and dark eyes. L: 11″, Wt: 1³/₄ oz.

The call note usually heard is a "brüb" or "prürr", uttered in various keys; a sharp "pitt" expresses anxiety. The song consists of a rhythmical "bick-bick-preerr".

◁ **Kingfisher** · *Alcedo atthis* (p. 23)

Distribution: Europe, chiefly the Mediterranean countries and east European steppe regions, roughly between longitude 10° W and 80° E, and between latitudes 30—50° N; however the Bee-eater does not breed in all parts of this area. It is also found in southern Africa. The Bee-eater is a rare visitor to Britain, but a pair tried to breed in Scotland in 1920, three pairs reared young in Sussex in 1955, while a pair bred in the Channel Isles the following year. The species is a summer visitor to Europe, spending the winter in dry open regions south of the Sahara.

Habitat: Bee-eaters like open country with few trees or bushes. For resting-perches they prefer thin twigs or telephone wires.

Breeding: Bee-eaters breed colonially in burrows which they dig in steep sand or earth banks, or sometimes even down into level ground. Hence one very often finds these birds near water where there are suitable banks or eroded creeks. The tunnels are dug by both partners in two to three weeks, and generally run horizontally into a bank, but slope down at an angle when excavated in flat ground. The tunnels are 1¹/₂—2 yds long and roughly 2 ins wide, terminating in a widened-out nest-chamber. No nest-material is used. As a rule the clutch consists of five or six eggs, pure white, nearly spherical and very thin-shelled, which are laid on the loose sand. Incubation is by both sexes, but chiefly the ♀. It generally takes a little over three weeks. The young fly when about four and a half weeks old. There is only one brood in a year.

Food: Almost exclusively insects caught on the wing in swallow-like fashion; in summer chiefly beetles, dragonflies, wasps and bees, also many cicadas. The prey is battered against a perch and then "nibbled" between the bird's mandibles, struggling all the time. This treatment makes the stings of those insects which have them "harmless", even though the bird makes no deliberate attempt to remove them.

Bee-eater · *Merops apiaster* ▷

◁ **Roller** · *Coracias garrulus* L.

Family: Rollers (Coraciidae)

Description: ♂ and ♀ are alike in colour: the mantle and back are chestnut, underside, head and neck are blue with greenish gloss. In flight the violet undersides of the secondaries are conspicuous. The young are duller in plumage, primarily because the blue of the underparts and head are tinged with brown. L: 12″ (Jackdaw-size), Wt: *c.* 5 oz.

The usual call is a harsh "rack" or "gack"; when agitated a crow-like "kraak" alarm note is used, and in display flights the ♂ gives a high "rerrerrerrerr". The young make almost continuous begging calls which sound like a mewing "yooi-yooi-yooi".

Distribution: Chiefly southern and eastern Europe and Asia east to 80°, northwards to latitude 60°. It also occurs in north Africa. The Roller is a summer visitor which goes to south Africa for the winter. It is only a rare visitor to Britain.

Habitat: Mostly open steppe-like country with tree-clumps or isolated trees containing holes; mature woods with clearings and rides, also (in open country) sandpits with holes in the excavated faces. Here several pairs sometimes breed in loose colonies.

Breeding: The ♂ has a most striking display flight in which it repeatedly tumbles through the air calling loudly and showing up the violet wing marks. For nesting holes the birds either choose ready-made sites (in trees, nestboxes, etc.) or else dig their own or enlarge tunnels made by Bee-eaters. Rollers do not build a nest, although the chosen hole sometimes contains an old nest of another species. Both sexes brood the four or five pure white eggs, which hatch in about 19 days. The young leave the nest after approximately four weeks. Single-brooded.

Food: The Roller sallies after its prey from perches such as treetops, posts and telephone wires. It feeds mainly on insects, especially large species such as grasshoppers, beetles, dragonflies and cicadas, which it picks off the ground or takes in flight. In addition it catches small vertebrates, e. g. mice, lizards, etc., which it kills with vigorous blows.

Hoopoe · *Upupa epops* L. ▷

Family: Hoopoes (Upupidae)

Description: The sexes are similar in colour. Most of the body plumage is pinkish-brown; the wings and tail are marked with alternate black and white bands. The erectile crest and the rather long, somewhat curved beak are unmistakable characters. L: 11", Wt: *c.* 2 oz.

The flight is quite slow and almost butterfly-like. The song is a very distinctive "poo-poo-poo". Also characteristic is a croaking alarm call.

Distribution: Nearly all Eurasia south of latitude 60°, and the continent of Africa. It is a summer visitor wintering mainly in savannah regions south of the Sahara. A few have been recorded spending the winter in southern Europe. The Hoopoe is a scarce visitor to Britain in spring and autumn, and breeds occasionally in southern counties.

Habitat: Open country with scattered trees or tree-clumps, also parkland, open woodland and treeless stony areas, as well as in and near villages (especially southern Europe).

Breeding: The Hoopoe breeds in holes in trees, walls, rock-faces, and sand or clay banks, also in nestboxes, and even in cracks in the ground and under boulders. The usual clutch consists of six eggs, brownish- or greenish-grey but often becoming stained; they are laid directly on the floor of the hole. Such nest material as is sometimes found in Hoopoes' holes is likely to have been taken in by other birds. The ♀ alone incubates, being fed by the ♂. Incubation takes 15—16 days, and fledging about another 26 days. Single-brooded.

Food: Predominantly insects and their larvae, especially dung-beetles, mole-crickets and grasshoppers.

◁ Wryneck · *Jynx torquilla* L.

Family: Woodpeckers (Picidae) *Subfamily:* Wrynecks (Jynginae)
Description: Both sexes have greyish-brown plumage with "scaly
bark" patterning. The underside is paler brown with darker barring.
Two of the four toes are directed forwards and two backwards. When
threatened the "Wryneck" twists head and neck in snake-like movements. L: 6¹/₃", Wt: *c.* 1¹/₄ oz.

The song is produced by both sexes, and often draws attention to the
birds; it is a nasal "weeweewee...". A high tinkling may be heard
from young birds.

Distribution: Most of Europe and large parts of Asia, roughly between
latitudes 50° and 60°, eastwards to the Pacific (southwards to about
30° N in east Asia). The Wryneck is absent from much of Spain and
from Morocco in north Africa, but also occurs in Algeria and Tunisia
north of the Sahara. The once sizeable southern British population has
enormously decreased, although migrant birds still occur. However,
Wrynecks recently bred for the first time in the eastern Highlands. The
Wryneck is a summer visitor, wintering principally in tropical Africa,
Persia and India.
Habitat: Parks, orchards and open deciduous woodland.

Breeding: On returning from its winter quarters the Wryneck repeats
its nasal calls near possible nesting sites. These are usually holes in trees
(especially old woodpecker holes), also nestboxes and sometimes holes
in walls. Both sexes are apparently involved in selecting a site, but in
most cases the ♂ seems to play the active role. The Wryneck builds
no nest, but throws out material (or eggs) belonging to other birds,
though sometimes leaving a thin layer in the hole. The clutch consists
of seven to ten (sometimes even more) pure white eggs, which are
incubated by both partners, but chiefly the ♀. The incubation period is
13—14 days. The young stay in the nest about three weeks, and after
flying are still tended for ten days or so. Normally one brood is reared
in a season, but second broods are on record.
Food: Almost exclusively ants and their pupae, largely species of
Lasius, Tetramorium and Myrmica.

34

Green Woodpecker · *Picus viridis* (L.) ▷

Family: Woodpeckers (Picidae) *Subfamily:* True woodpeckers (Picinae)
Description: Both sexes are moss-green above with a yellowish rump, and grey-green below; their crowns are red, the red area being larger in the ♂. At close range the colour of the moustachial stripes is a certain guide to the sex: in the ♀ the moustachial stripe and the area around the eye are uniformly black, whereas the ♂ has a red centre to the stripe. Juveniles have paler, lightly spotted upperparts and have dark streaking and barring underneath. L: 12^1/$_2$", Wt: *c.* 7 oz.

The Green Woodpecker's call, uttered by both sexes, is very distinctive. It consists of a repeated laughing "gewgewgew...". This species very rarely drums.

Distribution: England, Wales, lowland Scotland and all Europe, as far as about 60° N. The Green Woodpecker is also found in parts of Asia Minor, south-west Russia and west Persia. It is a resident.
Habitat: Open deciduous woodland, parks and orchards. Extends to an altitude of 5,000 ft on the Continent.

Breeding: Nest holes are normally excavated in deciduous trees. Exceptionally artificial sites are accepted. The clutch of five to eight pure white eggs is incubated by both partners for a period of rather over two weeks. The fledging period lasts about three weeks. The young are still dependent on the parents for another three weeks or so after leaving the nest. Normally single-brooded.
Food: Green and Grey-headed Woodpeckers feed largely on the ground, where they seek insects and their larvae. The Green Woodpecker's predilection is for ants' nests (especially in winter). In southern Europe it frequently attacks beehives, a habit occasionally also noted in Britain. In natural woodland, where dead trees (with the many grubs they contain) are not removed, it finds sufficient food even when there is deep snow, but this food source is largely lacking in plantations. Thus in severe winters with heavy snowfalls Green Woodpeckers may find next to no food and the population is sometimes decimated.

◁ **Grey-headed Woodpecker** · *Picus canus* Gmel.

Family: Woodpeckers (Picidae) *Subfamily:* True woodpeckers (Picinae)
Description: This species is rather like the Green Woodpecker and is often confused with it on the Continent. The most important differences from the latter are that both sexes have a grey head, there is only a little black in front of the eye and the blackish moustachial stripe is narrow. In the ♂ the forehead is red, while there is no red on the ♀ at all. Young birds resemble the adults in colour, although they are paler. L: 10″, Wt: 4¹/₂ oz.

♂ and ♀ produce a "song" similar to the Green Woodpecker's, but the notes are more musical and get deeper towards the end. This melancholy song, gradually slowing in tempo, is readily imitated.

Distribution: Middle and eastern Europe and southern Scandinavia roughly between the 50th and 60th latitudes as far as the Pacific and east Asia. The Grey-headed Woodpecker does not occur at all in the British Isles. It is a resident, and does not wander much.
Habitat: Chiefly hilly and mountainous areas, where it inhabits the same sorts of sites as the Green Woodpecker.

Breeding: In the early part of the breeding season the partners call to each other in the same way as Green Woodpeckers do. However these sessions are interspersed with vigorous "drumming". The general breeding biology also resembles the last species (q. v.). Single-brooded.
Food: While it is also a ground feeder, the Grey-headed Woodpecker is less of a specialist than the Green Woodpecker. In times of need it picks at carrion and fruit and visits bird tables. It is therefore less endangered than the latter species by hard winters. Grey-headed Woodpeckers are fond of unsalted fat or mixtures of equal parts of wheat bran and beef suet, as the photograph shows.

The Grey-headed Woodpecker is less aggressive than other woodpeckers. Where food is put out for them a male and a female may be seen in spring actually feeding amicably side by side.

Middle Spotted Woodpecker · *Dendrocopos medius* (L.) ▷

Family: Woodpeckers (Picidae) *Subfamily:* True woodpeckers (Picinae)
Description: ♂ and ♀ are blackish above with white shoulder-patches.
The wings are barred black and white, the white bands consisting of
rows of spots on the primaries. The whole crown is bright red, the
colour being paler and not extending so far back in the ♀. The underparts are off-white with dark streaks on the flanks, the whitish merg-
ing gradually with the dull pink colour of the belly. Juveniles resemble
the old birds but are paler. L: 2^1/$_4$″, Wt: *c.* 2 oz.

In spring the "song" of the ♂ may be heard, sounding like "gey
gey . . .". In addition both sexes have a "gick" note reminiscent of the
Great Spotted Woodpecker, and a rapidly repeated sequence of notes
like "kikiki . . .". The Middle Spotted Woodpecker seldom drums.

Distribution: Central Europe up to *c.* 55° N, eastwards to about as far
as the Urals, extreme north-west Spain, and from southern France to
south-east Europe, Asia Minor to Persia in scattered localities. It is
a resident.
Habitat: Chiefly open deciduous woods, parks and orchards. In oak-
hornbeam forest with old oaks the Middle Spotted Woodpecker is
often numerous. It is absent from pure conifer woods.

Breeding: Thick upward-sloping boughs are often chosen as sites for
the nest holes, with the entrance to the chamber sloping down at an
angle. Of course holes may also be bored in vertical trunks or branches. The clutch consists of four to six pure white eggs, which
are deposited directly on to the floor of the chamber (where there is
usually a layer of wood chippings). Incubation is shared by both sexes
and lasts 11—12 days. The young leave the hole after about three
weeks and are then tended by the parents for a further ten days or so.
Only one brood is reared in a year.
Food: All kinds of insects and their larvae, occasionally fruit, nuts,
seeds of trees, also food put out by man in winter (as described under
Grey-headed Woodpecker).

◁ **Lesser Spotted Woodpecker** · *Dendrocopos minor* (L.)

Family: Woodpeckers (Picidae) *Subfamily:* True woodpeckers (Picinae)
Description: This, easily the smallest European woodpecker, is rather like the last species in colour but lacks the white shoulder-patches. Instead there is white barring across the dark back. Furthermore there is no tinge of red on the underparts. While the ♂ has a red crown, this region is off-white in the ♀. Juveniles resemble the ♀, although ♂♂ have some red on the crown. L: *c.* 6″, Wt: *c.* 3/4 oz.

Both sexes produce a shrill "kikikikikiki" (heard especially in spring) recalling a Kestrel's call notes. Both partners also drum frequently.

Distribution: Most of England and Wales, all of mainland Europe, except for the most northerly parts, large parts of Asia (between 50° and 60° N to the Pacific), Algeria and Tunisia north of the Sahara as well as Asia Minor and north-west Persia. The Lesser Spotted Woodpecker is a resident.
Habitat: Orchards, parks, open lowland deciduous and mixed woodland.

Breeding: The birds call a lot in spring, and display flights and chases may be seen. Other members of the species entering the territory are vigorously driven out. Even while rearing young the partners easily become aggressive towards each other. Both sexes work to excavate the nest hole, which is in many cases high up in a dead branch of an old tree. However they occupy lower sites also, especially in orchards. The four or five pure white eggs take 11 days to hatch. The young fly after about three weeks and are tended by the parents for up to two more weeks. Single-brooded.
Food: This is similar to the Middle Spotted Woodpeckers's, although Lesser Spotted Woodpeckers only exceptionally take seeds and fruit. In summer many aphids and caterpillars are eaten. The principal winter nourishment comprises insects and grubs living or hibernating in timber. The birds open up galls eagerly but visit bird tables only occasionally.

Great Spotted Woodpecker · *Dendrocopos major* (L.) ▷

Family: Woodpeckers (Picidae) *Subfamily:* True woodpeckers (Picinae)
Description: The Great Spotted Woodpecker is, like the Middle Spotted, black and white; the under tail-coverts are red, contrasting sharply with the white belly. The head of the ♀ has no red at all, whereas the nape of the ♂ has a bright red patch. Juveniles are like the parents but the colour of the front part of the crown (in ♂♂ and ♀♀) is red. L: 9″, Wt: *c.* 2³/₄ oz.

The most noticeable call of this species is a sharp "chick", rapidly repeated when excited. An intensive drumming on dead branches largely replaces vocal courtship notes.

Distribution: The whole of Europe except Ireland and north Scandinavia; north Africa, Asia Minor and large parts of Asia, southwards to 20° N. The Great Spotted Woodpecker is a resident.
Habitat: Deciduous, mixed and conifer woods, parks and orchards, at all altitudes to the tree line.

Breeding: The nest chamber is hollowed out of deciduous or evergreen trees (in a dead or internally unsound part), the entrance hole being circular. Both partners take turns incubating the four to six pure white eggs, which takes 11—12 days. The young leave the hole after about three weeks, and are still taken care of for almost another fortnight. Single-brooded.
Food: As for Middle Spotted Woodpecker, also ripe fruit, nuts and seeds of trees (including pine), and sometimes young of other hole-nesting birds. In Britain the habit of visiting bird-tables is increasing.

Allied species: The Syrian Woodpecker *(Dendrocopos syriacus)* which lives in south-east Europe and western Asia is a very similar species to the above. The White-backed Woodpecker *(D. leucotus)* and the Three-toed Woodpecker *(Picoides tridactylus)* occur in northern Europe and locally in the Alps.

◁ **Black Woodpecker** · *Dryocopus martius* (L.)

Family: Woodpeckers (Picidae) *Subfamily:* True woodpeckers (Picinae)
Description: Both sexes have uniformly black plumage. In the ♂ the whole crown and in the ♀ the rear of the crown is red. The bill is yellow. This is the biggest European woodpecker. Juveniles are like the parents. L: 18″, Wt: *c.* 10½ oz.

The loud flight call, which sounds like "ripripriprip", is striking, and so is the "kleea" note made by birds at rest. In the breeding season there is also a "laughing" song; "quickwickwickwick". During changeover at the nest both partners produce a Jackdaw-like soft "jack".

Distribution: Central, eastern and northern Europe. In western and southern Europe it only occurs in high mountain ranges (e. g. the Pyrenees); it extends eastwards roughly between latitudes 50° and 65° N as far as the Pacific, also to the Caucasus and various mountainous parts of Turkey. It is a resident.
Habitat: Mainly extensive forests, predominantly coniferous, mixed or deciduous woods at moderate or high altitudes, locally also lowland woods.

Breeding: Nest holes are bored in the relatively branchless trunks of beeches and Scots pines, which are preferably isolated; holes are also often found in firs, more seldom in spruces. The vertically oval entrance is large enough for a human hand to reach in. The three to five pure white eggs are incubated by both partners for about 12 days. After approximately four weeks the young leave the hole but are still dependent on the parents for one to two months. Single-brooded.
Food: Chiefly insects and larvae which live in wood. The Black Woodpecker has a predilection for raiding ants' nests and in doing so drives large holes into fallen logs. In winter it sometimes uses wood-ants' mounds as a food source. It only exceptionally eats seeds and fruit.

Crested Lark · *Galerida cristata* (L.) ▷

Family: Larks (Alaudidae)

Description: Above, both ♂ and ♀ have irregular dark flecks and streaks on a grey-brown ground. There are dark streaks on the greyish-white underparts, especially in the throat region. Both sexes have a pointed crest on the head. Juveniles are like adults in colour, but with the addition of dirty white flecks on the upper parts. The wing-coverts and flight feathers have pale edges. L: 6³/₄″, Wt: 1²/₃ oz.

Crested Larks utter a plaintive "dri-dri-drioo" during flight. The song is shorter than the Skylark's, with similar rippling and subdued notes, but also flute-like elements. Other birds' songs are frequently incorporated. The Crested Lark usually sings perched on a stone or low bush, sometimes also in heavy fluttering flight.

Distribution: The whole of continental Europe as far as 60° N, large areas of Asia, south of latitude 50° to Korea, from Asia Minor to north-west India, the Arabian peninsula and large stretches of Africa above 10° N. The Crested Lark is a resident, and shows little movement. Extremely few have ever wandered to Britain.

Habitat: Open, more or less treeless country, many semi-desert areas in southern Europe, but also near habitations and vineyards. This species favours airfields and race-tracks locally, and avoids high mountains. Since the end of the war it has become rare or even vanished in certain areas.

Breeding: The nest is placed in slight depressions in the ground, under grass tussocks, on slagheaps, verges of tracks and similar sites. Little art goes into its construction of straws and rootlets, lined with finer stems. The four or five eggs have a whitish ground heavily speckled with greyish-brown. As a rule only the ♀ incubates. The young hatch in about 13 days and after nine or ten days leave the nest before they are able to fly. They become independent after about four weeks. Double-brooded.

Food: Chiefly weed seeds, soft parts of plants, also smaller insects such as grasshopper nymphs.

Allied species:
The Thekla Lark *(Galerida theklae)*, which inhabits southern France, Spain, Portugal and north Africa is very similar to the Crested Lark. It has narrower breast-streaks and a shorter, thicker bill; its song is more whistling.

◁ **Woodlark** · *Lullula arborea* (L.) Above

Family: Larks (Alaudidae)
Description: Both sexes are greyish-brown above with dark flecking, and whitish to creamy below with fine dark streaks, especially on the breast. The whitish eye-stripes, which meet on the nape, are noticeable. L: 6″.
   A musical "titlooee" is often heard from Woodlarks in flight. The song, with its flute-like, descending phrases like "loodl-loodl-loodl-lululululululu" is very beautiful and characteristic.

Distribution: All of Europe to about 60° N, north Africa, Asia Minor, eastwards to longitude 60°. It breeds only in the southern part of Britain, where it seems to be largely resident. On the continent it is a partial migrant, largely wintering around the Mediterranean.
Habitat: Dry woodland edge, heathland and dry slopes with a few trees, also stony country with sparse vegetation (particularly in southern Europe and some mountain regions).

Breeding: In its breeding biology it resembles the Crested Lark. The three to five eggs have rather dense, fine brownish speckling on a whitish ground. Like all larks the young leave the nest before they can fly. Usually double-brooded.
Food: Weed seeds, soft parts of plants and many smallish insects.

◁ **Shore Lark** · *Eremophila alpestris* (L.) Below

Family: Larks (Alaudidae)
Description: Upperparts greyish-brown, underparts dirty white. The

throat and forehead are pale yellow, and the throat is sharply bounded by a black breast-band. The cheeks are black, and the arms of a black crescent across the crown run back to terminate in two small "horns" in the nape region. The plumage of the ♀ is paler, with less black. Juveniles resemble the ♀. L: 6¼", Wt: nearly 1½ oz. ♀♀ are somewhat lighter in weight.

The call is a metallic-sounding "zee-tee". The ♂ sings its tinkling, musical song both from the ground and while circling high in the air.

Distribution: Northernmost Scandinavia , the north of the Soviet Union to Siberia, high mountain ranges in central Asia, Persia, Turkey, north and north-east Africa, north-west Arabia and North America. In southern Europe it is only known in Greece. On passage it may occur in any part of Europe. It is a partial migrant, often wintering in middle and southern Europe. Small numbers winter on the east coast of Britain.

Habitat: In winter chiefly sea coasts, sometimes also fields and meadows. In the breeding season it inhabits mountains above the tree-line, or tundra in the far north.

Breeding: As with larks generally, nests are well hidden on the ground, and the breeding biology is much like that of others of the family.

Food: Mainly insects during the breeding season, but also weed seeds, which form the mainstay at migration time; small molluscs are also taken occasionally.

Skylark · *Alauda arvenis* L. ▷

Family: Larks (Alaudidae)
Description: ♂ and ♀ are brown above, with dark flecks and streaks; most of the underside is whitish but the sandy-coloured throat region is streaked blackish-brown. The wing feathers are dark brown with pale edges, and the outer vanes of the outermost tail feathers are white. Juveniles are like the adults, although they look more "chequered" because of the rusty brown margins of their white-tipped back feathers. L: 7", Wt: *c.* 1⅓ oz.

The Skylark's flight-note is "tirrup". Its long-sustained song is made up of shrill trilling sequences, of limited musical range but full of variation, and is frequently interspersed with imitations of other birds. Now and then it is uttered from a perch, but usually in hovering song-flight, ♂♂ rising until they sometimes look like mere specks in the sky. Skylarks singing while "suspended" high in the air form part of the characteristic picture of the open countryside in spring.

Distribution: All of Europe, except for the extreme north, and southern Greece; on eastwards to Japan and the coast of the Bering Sea. The Skylark also occurs in southern Russia and in north Africa. It is a partial migrant which winters in the milder parts of western Europe and the Mediterranean area.

Habitat: Agricultural land, waste ground with low vegetation, grassland and extensive marshy meadows, as well as moorland where it often extends far above the tree limit.

Breeding: During early spring the ♂♂ perform tireless song-flights and mark out the bounds of their territories. In addition the peculiar ground display may be seen in March and April, the ♂ dancing round the ♀ with drooped wings. The simple nest is, in usual lark fashion, well hidden on the ground. As a rule the ♀ alone incubates the three to six eggs, for 11—14 days. The young leave the nest when still flightless after nine or ten days. Normally double-brooded.

Food: Predominantly weed seeds, grass shoots and other soft plant food, also small insects in the breeding season. In the winter months Skylarks are not very choosy; they often dig food out from under the snow, and will feed in stable manure.

Allied species:
A further 5 species of lark breed in Europe: in Mediterranean countries the stout-billed Calandra Lark *(Melanocorypha calandra);* and two similarly thick-billed species, mainly resident in central Asia but extending westwards to 40° longitude, are the White-winged Lark *(M. leucoptera)* which has a white wing-bar, and the Black Lark *(M. yeltoniensis).*
The Short-toed Lark *(Calandrella brachydactyla)* and the Lesser Short-toed Lark *(C. rufescens),* are the two smallest larks in the western Mediterranean area, north Africa and Asia.

House Martin · *Delichon urbica* (L.) Above ▷

Family: Swallows (Hirundinidae)
Description: Both sexes have glossy blue-black upperparts, while the entire underparts and the rump are pure white. The legs have white feathering right down to the toes. Juveniles are like the parents but their plumage is dingier. There is a suggestion of an indistinct greyish-brown band at the sides of the breast. L: 5″, Wt: *c.* ²/₃ oz.

The House Martin's song is a weak gossipy twittering; its call note is a chirping "chirrip", becoming a hoarse "seer" when excited.

Distribution: All Europe except the extreme north-east, large areas of Asia as far as Japan, and north Africa. It is a summer visitor, spending the winter in west, east and southern Africa.
Habitat: The House Martin is found close to buildings, whether in towns, villages or isolated; it also quite often lives far from habitations in rocky ravines or by cliffs. It is a sociable bird, frequently breeding in sizeable colonies.

Breeding: Nests are made from mud or clay, under eaves of buildings or in similar sites, while in some districts (including many British localities) sites under cliff-overhangs are much used. Very often several nests are joined together. They are lined with a little grass and feathers. The three to six pure white eggs are incubated by both partners for 14—15 days. The young leave the nest after about 28 days, although after this they are still repeatedly guided back by the parents for feeding. Two broods a year are reared in most areas.
Food: As for other hirundines.

Remarks: The species can often be induced to breed in a particular area by the erection of artificial nests.

Sand Martin · *Riparia riparia* (L.) Below ▷

Family: Swallows (Hirundinidae)
Description: Both sexes are earth-brown above and white with a

55

brown breast-band below; the tail is slightly forked. Young birds resemble the parents. L: 4³/₄″, Wt: *c.* ¹/₂ oz.

The usual call heard from these very social birds is a dry "chrrr", which also forms part of the twittering song.

Distribution: The whole of Europe and nearly all Asia, where it is only lacking in the extreme north and south of latitude 25°, also over almost the entire North American continent from Alaska to Mexico. It is a summer visitor, the European population wintering chiefly in east Africa.
Habitat: Sand Martins like open country. They prefer the surroundings of rivers and pools (and, locally, sea-coasts) with sandy banks, but also occur at sandpits and other soft banks far from water.

Breeding: Nesting burrows, 1¹/₂—3 ft in length, are dug out by the birds themselves, which place their nests in oven-shaped enlargements at the end. They consist of straws and rootlets, lined with feathers. The clutch of five or six pure white eggs is incubated for 12—16 days, by both partners. The young fly in 16—22 days. One or two broods per year.
Food: Predominantly small flying insects.

◁ **Swallow** · *Hirundo rustica* L.

Family: Swallows (Hirundinidae)
Description: Both sexes are a glossy dark blue above. The chin and throat are brick-red, separated by a bluish-black band from the remaining underparts which are creamy. The elongated outer feathers give the forked tail its graceful form. Juveniles resemble the old birds, but are more drab and lack the long tail-streamers. L: 7¹/₂″, Wt: ²/₃ oz.

Swallows draw attention to themselves by their "witt-witt" calls. The song, often given from telephone wires or a dead branch, is a musical babble composed of twittering and buzzing notes. When alarmed they give a sharp "biwist".

Distribution: Similar to the House Martin's in Europe, Asia and north Africa, also found over much of North America, from Alaska to Mexico. It is very familiar to all country-folk in Britain. In some parts of Europe there appears to have been a recent decline in numbers. It is a summer visitor, which winters in India and Africa south of latitude 12° N (British birds go to South Africa).

Habitat: Mainly cultivated land with farms and villages, but in southern Europe also far from human habitations. It is less sociable than other hirundines.

Breeding: The open nest is built in barns (especially where there are livestock), outbuildings and porches; in southern Europe also under eaves of buildings and under bridges, as well as in mine-shafts and caves. The nest is of mud and straw lined with feathers, and there is a characteristic gap of about 2 ins between its rim and the ceiling. The three to seven white eggs, heavily spotted with reddish-brown, are brooded very largely by the ♀, and hatch in 12—18 days, depending on temperature. The young fly when about three weeks old, and perch on nearby twigs or wires waiting to be fed. They return to the nest to roost, and sometimes also to be fed. Usually two, sometimes three broods a year.

Food: Chiefly small flies, horseflies and similar insects.

Allied species:

Two further hirundine species breed in Europe.

The Red-rumped Swallow *(Hirundo daurica)*, like a Swallow with a rust-red rump, is found in Spain and Greece.

The Crag Martin *(H. rupestris)* is superficially like a Sand Martin but has an unforked tail with a row of white spots; it inhabits rocky areas from the Alps southwards.

Golden Oriole · *Oriolus oriolus* (L.), ♀ left, ♂ right ▷

Family: Orioles (Oriolidae)

Description: The whole body of the ♂ is brilliant yellow, wings and tail being mainly black. In the ♀ the upperparts are greyish-green as far as

the yellowish-green rump, and the wings and tail are olive-grey, the latter tipped yellow. Her underparts are greyish-white with yellow-tinged flanks and dark streaking on the throat, breast and flanks. Juveniles look like the ♀. Young ♂♂ only become yellow in their third year. L: 9½″, Wt: 2½ oz.

The rich far-carrying calls of the ♂, "deedeedeleelioh" are used to demonstrate territory-ownership, whereas the much less striking song—a subdued chattering usually uttered near the future nest site, may well have something to do with indicating the chosen site. But it could also simply be "conversational", without specific function. Both sexes show agitation by a harsh "chrray" and fear by a snarling "krr". Young birds, and also the brooding ♀, have a nasal "guckuck" note.

Distribution: The European mainland, in the north to latitude 60°, to 100° E in Asia, southwards to India, Asia Minor, Persia and north-west Africa. In mountain regions it occurs up to altitudes of 2,000 ft, rarely higher. It occasionally nests in southern Britain. The Golden Oriole is a summer visitor, which winters mainly in eastern and southern Africa, migrating south in August and September.
Habitat: Parkland, lowland woods (deciduous and coniferous), also orchards with old trees.

Breeding: On fine days in late April and early May the loud, melodious calls of the ♂♂, of which several often court one ♀, may be heard. The nest (plate p. 236, lower) is well hidden, usually high up in the crown of a large tree. The clutch of three to five eggs, seldom larger, is normally incubated by the ♀ alone, although there are occasional observations of a ♂ sitting. Incubation lasts 14—15 days, and after fully two week the young leave the nest. Only one brood per year.
Food: Largely insects, above all caterpillars and butterflies, and also juicy fruit like cherries, berries and pears.

Raven · *Corvus corax* L. (Illustration follows p. 63)

Family: Crows (Corvidae)
Description: ♂ and ♀ are uniformly black, the plumage having a slight

gloss. The powerful bill and wedge-shaped tail are noticeable features. Juveniles are like their parents but, being duller, their plumage tends to appear browner. L: 24¹/₂″, Wt: 2—2¹/₂ lb.

The usual calls given by Ravens are a deep "pruk" and a high-pitched "klock", also a variety of guttural sounds. When excited they use a harsh "krack-krack". They often imitate the voices of animals living near them, in a deep-bellied chatter. Captive Ravens learn to repeat phrases well enough for their voices to be taken for human.

Distribution: Europe from Gibraltar to the North Cape, except for large regions of central Europe where it has been exterminated; Asia down to 30° N, Asia Minor, Arabia and Africa north of the Equator; North America and the coasts of Greenland. The Raven is a resident, which does not wander much; flocks may be seen where it is common. In Britain it occurs mainly in the west and north.
Habitat: Wild, open hill and mountain country and rocky coasts, also at times wooded heath and hill ground, even tundra. Intensively cultivated land is avoided.

Breeding: Ravens pair for life and are faithful to a nest site for many years. In late winter they begin their noisy aerobatic display. The nest is built on a cliff ledge beneath an overhang, or in a big tree, and even on the ground in treeless uninhabited regions. It is of variable size, sturdily constructed of sticks, the cup softly lined with wool, animal hair, grass or lichens. The clutch is formed of three to six eggs, which have olive-green and dark brown markings on a bluish-green ground. Only the ♀ incubates, and is fed with food the ♂ brings in its throat-pouch. After 20—21 days the young hatch, and fly about 45 days later. The family still remains together for several months. Young birds first come into breeding condition at two years. Single-brooded.
Food: Ravens are omnivorous, eating insects, worms, snails, carrion and any animals they are able to kill themselves. Local habits consist of probing in cowpats for beetle-larvae in late summer, and the visiting of refuse heaps in parties in winter. Sheep-carrion is extensively taken where available.

Raven · *Corvus corax* ▷

Above: breeding plumage; Below: juvenile

Family: Crows (Corvidae)

Description: ♂ and ♀ are black all over, with faint gloss. The bill is less powerful than the Raven's, and the end of the tail is straight, not wedge-shaped. Young birds resemble the parents but have no gloss. Young crows also have blue-grey eyes, the adults' being blackish-brown. L: 18¹/₂″, Wt: *c.* 1¹/₄ lb.

Both in flight and from perches (when each note is often accompanied by a bow) their usual call is a harsh "kaark"; there is also a shrill "krik" and a snarling "quarr" when mobbing birds of prey. The song is a low-pitched bubbling. In captivity it learns to mimic strange sounds and to repeat words.

Distribution: Western Europe, eastwards to about as far as the Elbe; northwards to Denmark and Scotland except the northern Highlands, very rare in Ireland. South of the Alps the edge of its range runs from the eastern Maritime Alps along the northern edge of the plain of the Po to the eastern approaches of the Alps, and from here on almost exactly northwards. On both sides of this boundary is a broad zone of interbreeding with the Hooded race, where hybrids from the almost black to types very like the Hooded Crow occur. Such intermediate plumage phases are common in parts of the Scottish Highlands. The Carrion Crow is a resident.

Habitat: Farmland with hedgerow timber or copses, moorland, small woods, also around villages and in parks. In some mountainous areas it breeds at altitudes of 6,500 ft.

Breeding: As a rule the birds pair in February and March, even earlier in mild weather. Once paired, Crows usually remain together for life or at least several years. In autumn and winter Carrion Crows quite often form flocks, which break up again at the winter's end. Only immature and unmated birds stay in smaller parties through the summer. Crows gain sexual maturity when two years old, but usually first breed in their third summer. Nests are generally built in stout forks well up in trees, but where there are no trees the crows use bushes or crags; ground nests are quite exceptional. Carrion Crows tend to stick to their territory and may return to their old nest, which they merely repair. New nests are usually built close to the previous site. Pairs always breed alone, defending their territory against others of their kind. The two to six eggs (plate p. 236, upper) are incubated by the ♀ alone (starting with the first egg) and begin to hatch in 18—19 days. The young leave the nest after 31—32 days but still stay with the parents for a number of weeks. Single-brooded.

Food: The species is omnivorous, eating both grain and animal food. It robs a great many nests. Where it is not kept down by gamekeepers it becomes very common because its natural enemies have declined. In winter it often visits rubbish dumps in flocks.

Remarks: The Crow has two superficially very distinct subspecies or colour phases: 1. Carrion Crow (see p. 66), 2. Hooded Crow (see below).

Hooded Crow · *Corvus corone cornix* L. ▷

Family: Crows (Corvidae)

Description: The sexes are alike. The lower neck, back, breast and belly are grey, the rest of the body is black as in the Carrion Crow. Juveniles look like the parents. The Hooded Crow's calls are just like the Carrion Crow's. The size and weight are as in the latter race.

Distribution: The main range is to the east of the boundaries given for the Carrion Crow; it is found as far as the Pacific coast and Japan, and southwards to 30° N; in Europe it extends to the North Cape. The Hooded Crow replaces the Carrion Crow in Ireland, the Isle of Man and northern Scotland. Hybrids occur wherever the two forms meet. The Hooded Crow is a partial migrant which moves westwards in winter, reaching central France. At this time it can be seen associating with Carrion Crows at rubbish dumps. Many winter on the coast, feeding along the tideline. Some birds come to eastern England in winter, but far fewer than formerly.

Habitat, Breeding and *Food* are all as in the Carrion Crow.

◁ **Rook** · *Corvus frugilegus* L.

Family: Crows (Corvidae)

Description: Both sexes are uniformly black with purplish gloss. Adult birds have bare, white and scaly skin at the base of the bill. In young birds, which have duller plumage, the base of the bill is feathered. This makes them easily mistakable for Carrion Crows. However Rooks' bills are narrower, with less curvature, and the feathers on the upper part of the leg give a "baggy pants" appearance. The purple gloss, especially on head and neck, is also very noticeable; Carrion Crows lack this. L: 18″, Wt: *c.* 1 lb.

The characteristic note of the Rook is a deep raucous "kraah", appreciably deeper than that of the Crow. The song is a deep-pitched "crackling".

Distribution: Central and western Europe (including the whole British Isles), north to southern Scandinavia, south to the Alps with a pocket in the western Pyrenees, and a narrow zone from the eastern Danube basin to eastern Greece; also large areas of Asia between latitudes 30° and 60°. British Rooks are resident, but those from colder areas move to western and southern Europe in winter.

Habitat: Open ground with woods and copses. In many places the birds also breed in parkland.

Breeding. Rooks are social birds and usually breed in sizeable colonies. The noise the birds make draws attention to these rookeries. The nests are generally a few yards apart, but sometimes they even touch each other. They are generally placed well out on branches at the tops of high trees, built of sticks and lined with vegetable matter rather than wool or hair. British birds settle in their colonies in March, when northern and eastern birds are starting their homeward migration. The ♂ selects the nest site and shows it to the ♀, adopting characteristic postures. The clutch consists of three to six eggs, which resemble those of the Crow. Only the ♀ incubates, while the ♂ brings food to her. Incubation lasts 17—20 days; the young leave the nest when barely five weeks old and follow the parents for some weeks afterwards. The birds remain social after the breeding season and form even bigger flocks in autumn. Young birds attain sexual maturity in their second summer (rarely before). As a rule, Rooks pair for life. Single-brooded.

Food: The Rook is, like all corvids, omnivorous, although it takes a higher proportion of vegetable food than the other species. The animal food which is eaten includes harmful insect larvae and even mice, and this possibly counterbalances the harm done to crops. It is therefore protected in some parts of the Continent.

Alpine Chough · *Pyrrhocorax graculus* (L.) ▷

Family: Crows (Corvidae)

Description: ♂♂ and ♀♀ are uniformly black with slight gloss; they have orange-red legs and a pale yellow bill. Juveniles resemble the parents but have black legs. L: 15″.

Alpine Choughs attract notice by their loud "cheeup" whistles and rolling "kreeerr" calls. Harsh "kraah" calls indicate alarm. The song is a croaking chatter. They are very acrobatic in flight.

Distribution: The whole area of the Alps and the high mountains of Greece, Italy, Corsica and Spain; also the mountain ranges of north-west Africa, western Asia, the Himalayan region and west China.

Habitat: Alpine Choughs are characteristic birds of high mountains and live mainly above the tree limit. In southern Europe somewhat lower wild rocky country is also inhabited. In winter they descend as far as the valleys.

Breeding: Alpine Choughs are social birds and mostly nest colonially in niches and holes in steep cliffs, sometimes also in caves and buildings. The nest is of large twigs, softly lined with hair and wool. Knowledge of its breeding biology is sketchy. The clutch consists of three to five eggs, whitish with brownish streaks. Incubation takes 18—21 days. The young fly after about 31 days, and then stay with the parents for quite some time afterwards. Single-brooded.

Food: Insects (grasshoppers and beetles), spiders, worms, small vertebrates. Rowan berries and fruit are eaten in autumn. In winter flocks

often visit climbing huts and hotels to feed on kitchen scraps, also becoming sufficiently tame to accept food from tourists there.

Allied species:
The Chough *(Pyrrhocorax pyrrhocorax)* is rather similar to the Alpine Chough but is glossier and has red legs and bill (the latter being rather long and decurved). Juveniles have orange bills. The commonest call is a ringing, drawn-out "kyah". This species is a resident in coastal regions of Ireland (except the east) and locally in west Wales, the Isle of Man and the Inner Hebrides; in these regions it chiefly frequents coastal cliffs, but also ruins, cliffs and quarries inland. Abroad it breeds in Brittany, Iberia, the Alps, the Mediterranean region, northwest Africa and parts of Asia. It extends less far up the mountains than the Alpine Chough. In nest sites and breeding biology it generally resembles the latter species. However, six eggs are sometimes laid and it is known that only the ♀ incubates, while fledging takes over five weeks. The diet is mainly of insects, but crustaceans, molluscs, worms and even lizards are taken too, and also corn at times.

Jackdaw · *Corvus monedula* L. (Illustration follows p. 75)

Family: Crows (Corvidae)
Description: Both sexes are glossy black above and blackish-grey below; the nape and cheeks are grey. The black bill is fairly short. The eyes are pale grey. Juveniles resemble the adults. L: 13", Wt: c. 8 oz.

The Jackdaw can be recognised by its shrill "jack" call, at times rapidly repeated. Hoarse "kraah" or "caaw" calls are given when excited. In captivity Jackdaws learn to imitate various noises and to repeat words. Their song is a crackling chattering.

Distribution: Europe, to latitude 60° N, eastwards to 100° E, northwest Africa. Jackdaws are partial migrants, some parts of the population making considerable movements within Europe outside the breeding season.

Habitat: Jackdaws are equally at home among cliffs and steep-sided ravines, ruins and buildings, and in parks and open woodland, wherever there are suitable nesting holes. In some areas holes in the banks of sandpits are much used.

Breeding: Jackdaws are social birds and generally breed in colonies. Nests are normally built inside a cavity (but occasionally in quite an exposed site) of sticks with a soft lining of hair, rags, feathers, etc. The twigs to be used are usually broken off branches by the birds themselves. The three to six eggs have a pale blue ground colour with greyish-brown spots, and are normally brooded by the ♀. The ♂ feeds her, and on exceptional occasions may relieve her on the nest for a short time. Incubation takes 17—19 days, and the fledging period is 30—35 days, after which the young still remain with the parents for some time. After the breeding season Jackdaws move about in flocks. Single-brooded.

Food: Jackdaws are omnivorous and feed in the same places as Rooks, though taking their food from the surface instead of probing. A few birds become habitual nest-robbers. In winter they often associate with Rooks in flocks on farmland or rubbish dumps.

Magpie · *Pica pica* (L.) (Illustration precedes p. 78)

Family: Crows (Corvidae)
Description: ♂ and ♀ are, except for the white belly and two white shoulder-patches, black with bluish iridescence on the flight feathers and a greenish, slightly bronze sheen on the tail feathers. Juveniles resemble adults, but are less bright. L: 18″ (of which about half is tail), Wt: *c.* 7¹/₂ oz.

The Magpie is very noisy, and its chattering "chackchackchack" is frequently heard. Young birds have a husky "chirrack" begging note. The Magpie's gurgling song is in part quite musical. Pet birds reared from the nestling stage learn to repeat words.

Jackdaw · *Corvus monedula* ▷

Distribution: The Magpie is found all over Europe and in large parts of Asia. It occurs eastwards right to the Pacific coast, as well as in north Africa and over large areas of North America, especially the western states. It is a resident.

Habitat: The Magpie likes open cultivated land with trees and hedges. It also occurs in lowland woods, parkland and even in urban areas. On the continent it is sometimes found on alpine meadows adjoined by tree-clumps, scrub or open woodland, up to 6,000 ft. It breeds on a number of islands off the coast of Britain and Ireland.

Breeding: Nests are built in trees or tall hedges (especially thorn hedges). The outer framework of sticks includes a dome over the nest-cup, which is formed of mud lined with rootlets, hair, etc. More often than not a new nest is built each year. Only the ♀ incubates the four to eight (rarely more or fewer) eggs, which are light green with fairly dense greyish-brown spotting. The incubation period is about 21 days, starting well before clutch completion. The young fly when 25—27 days old, but remain under parental care for a considerable further period. Normally single-brooded; repeats after failures are frequent.

Food: Like others of the family the Magpie is omnivorous. It is an inveterate robber of eggs and young birds and is therefore persecuted by game preservers. In parts of Europe the bird has increased in numbers following the decline in the Goshawk and Peregrine, its natural enemies.

Allied species:
The smaller Azure-winged Magpie *(Cyanopica cyanus)* breeds in southern Spain and Portugal and also in east Asia. It may be told by its black crown, blue wings and tail, and pale body.

◁ **Magpie** · *Pica pica* (p. 75)

Siberian Jay · *Perisoreus infaustus* (L.) Above ▷

Family: Crows (Corvidae)
Description: The sexes are alike in colour. The crown is dark brown, the entire upperparts are greyish-brown. The paler underside is rust- to mouse-grey; under tail-coverts, rump and outer tail feathers are fox-red. Juveniles resemble adults. L: *c.* 12″.
   A rasping Jay-like call and a mewing note are frequently uttered.

Distribution: Scandinavia, north-east Europe and much of Asia between latitudes 50° and 70° N. The Siberian Jay is predominantly resident.
Habitat: Northern coniferous and birch forests. Outside the breeding season it shows confidence towards human beings.

Breeding: The stout nest is generally built close against a tree-trunk. The three to five greenish-white eggs with grey-brown spots are like small pale Magpie eggs. Little is known about the bird's breeding biology.
Food: Insects and tree seeds are eaten among the twigs in tit-like acrobatics. Small vertebrates and scraps are also taken.

Jay · *Garrulus glandarius* (L.) Below ▷

Family: Crows (Corvidae)
Description: Both sexes are mainly cinnamon-brown, with a white rump and fine black and white streaks along the front part of the crown. Thick black moustachial stripes border the white throat. The flight feathers are blackish, each wing has a white patch and coverts mostly blue with black barring. The tail is black. Young birds resemble the adults but the contrast in colours is less marked.
L: 13³/₄″, Wt: 6 oz.
   The Jay's loud screech is characteristic. It also has various chuckling notes and a mewing is often heard which is confusingly like a Buzzard's. The song is a soft guttural babbling.

Distribution: The whole of Europe except the extreme north; Asia Minor, south-west Russia, west Persia, large regions of Asia as far as Japan, also north Africa. The Jay is a partial migrant, northern birds to some extent wintering in mid- and south Europe.

Habitat: Broad-leaved and mixed woods, also conifer woods or plantations, and parkland; in south Europe it favours pine and cork-oak woods. In places it extends into orchards and suburban areas.

Breeding: The nest is often placed close to the trunk of a tree, or else in a small fork. It is made of twigs, lined with rootlets. The four to seven eggs, pale green with dense grey-brown freckling, hatch after 16—18 days' incubation. The young fly when about 20 days old. Normally single-brooded.

Food: Jays are omnivorous. In the breeding season they rob nests on a large scale. In autumn they feed on acorns and nuts.

◁ **Nutcracker** · *Nucifraga caryocatactes* (L.)

Family: Crows (Corvidae)

Description: ♂ and ♀ are alike in plumage. The crown is blackish-brown, most of the body grey-brown with white spots, the wings being blackish and the under tail-coverts snow-white. The tail is black with a white terminal band below. Juvenile plumage is similar. L: 12¼", Wt: *c.* 7 oz.

The most striking call is a repeated "krorkrorkrorkror . . .". A soft "krrr", presumed to have a warning function, is also heard. The song is a gurgling chatter.

Distribution: Hill or mountain regions of central and eastern Europe, southern Scandinavia, north-east Europe and much of Asia between 40° and 70° N, round to Japan and the Himalayas. The Nutcracker is mainly resident. In certain winters the Siberian race erupts south-westwards, some birds occasionally reaching Britain.

Habitat: Upland coniferous woods. At high population densities it may overflow locally into mixed woodland.

Breeding: Early layings may occur at the beginning of March, but the beginning of April is the normal time for first eggs. The nest is well hidden, generally against a trunk. It is decorated with lichens. The three or four eggs, pale greenish-white with brownish markings, are incubated entirely by the ♀, which is fed during this period by the ♂ close to the nest. The incubation period is 17—19 days and the fledging period 23—25 days. Normally one brood is raised in a year, although the not infrequent appearance of newly-fledged young in late summer gives rise to suspicion of some second broods. However these may simply be from repeat broods. There has been little detailed work on the Nutcracker's breeding biology.

Food: Chiefly hazel-nuts and seeds of Arolla pine, other conifers, oak, beech, etc. Insects (especially beetles), fruit and sometimes even kitchen scraps are also taken. This species only occasionally preys on nests or small vertebrates.

Great Tit · *Parus major* L.
(Flight illustrations: further illustration after p. 87) ▷

Family: Tits (Paridae)
Description: The upperparts are mainly greenish-grey, the head black with white cheeks, and the underparts bright yellow with a black stripe from throat to vent. The wings and tail are predominantly grey. The ♀ is less bright than the ♂ and has a narrower breast-stripe. The young resemble adults, apart from having yellowish cheeks and blackish-brown heads. L: 5½", Wt: c. ⅔ oz.

The Great Tit has a wide range of notes. The song is loud and can hardly be missed; the form heard especially in spring is the 'saw-sharpening' "teecher teecher". Another variation sounds like "ziziday". In addition there are numerous calls, including a sharp "pink", a querulus "zi-twit", a scolding "settetet" when agitated. Great Tits also imitate other birds frequently.

Distribution: The Great Tit inhabits all of Europe except the extreme north, almost all of Asia below 60° N, southwards to Indonesia, also north Africa. It is the most widely distributed of the tits. It is a partial migrant, some Continental birds moving southwards for the winter.

Habitat: Woodland (but scarce in pure conifer woods), parks, orchards and gardens even in towns. Common in lowland areas; in the Alps it extends locally to 5,000 ft above sea level.

Breeding: Great Tits are—like all true tits—hole-nesters. But they are not choosey and will build in tree-holes, nestboxes, holes in walls, rock banks or under eaves, squirrels' dreys, and odd sites like letterboxes. The ♂♂ already sing a great deal in winter. Nest building begins in late March or early April. For this they collect chiefly moss, animal hair and wool, but where moss is in short supply grass stalks may be used. The deep cup is softly lined with hair or wool. The ♂ as a rule takes no part in building, merely accompanying the ♀. The clutch consists of seven to thirteen (usually about ten) eggs, white with fine red-brown spots. Before incubation starts the ♀ always covers the eggs with nest material when leaving the nest; once incubation begins she no longer does this. The ♀ does all the incubating; when surprised on the nest she makes hissing noises. Incubation as a rule takes 12—14 days, although periods from 10—18 days have been recorded. The young normally stay in the nest for 19 days; they can leave earlier if disturbed. After flying they are still dependent on the parents for one to two weeks. The mortality rate among juvenile tits is very high. One brood per year is the rule, but in years of abundant food two may be raised, especially in coniferous woods.

Food: Insects and their larvae and eggs, also spiders and centipedes; caterpillars are preferred. In autumn and winter the birds take seeds (especially those rich in fat), animal and vegetable fat, also soft fruit.

Great Tits and most of the other true tits readily take possession of nestboxes put up for them. They are attracted to bird-tables, and sometimes even enter larders, where for preference they peck into packets of butter or margarine. The opening of milk-bottle tops is a recently formed habit in Britain.

Great Tit · *Parus major* (p. 83) Above ▷

Marsh Tit · *Parus palustris* L. (Further illustration precedes p. 94) Below ▷

Family: Tits (Paridae)

Description: It has uniformly grey-brown upperparts, glossy black crown, and matt off-white underparts; there is a black patch on the chin. The wings and tail are grey-brown. Juveniles resemble adults but the black on the head lacks gloss. L: $4^1/_2''$, Wt: $^2/_5$ oz.

The Marsh Tit's characteristic song is a rattling "chepchepchepchep..." which it can deliver at varying rates. A sharp "pitchoo" is also often heard, and a chattering "chickadeedeedeedee" is used when excited.

Distribution: Europe as far north as 65° and southwards to latitude 40°, otherwise only in east Asia, the two populations being isolated from each other as far as is known. It occurs all over England and Wales and very locally in southern Scotland, but not in Ireland. Outside the breeding season the Marsh Tit does not usually move about much.

Habitat: Deciduous and mixed woodland (mainly lowland), also parks and orchards. Dark pine and fir woods are avoided. It is not restricted to marshy areas.

Breeding: Nests are similar in construction to those of Great and other tits, although in some sites there is room for very little material. The Marsh Tit uses a similar variety of sites, but prefers natural holes in trees. The six to ten eggs look like Great Tits' except for their smaller size and finer speckling. Incubation is by the ♀ only and normally takes 12—13 days. The fledging period is 17—20 days. Single-brooded as a rule.

Food: Similar to other tits.

Allied Species:

There are three other European species of tits which are somewhat like the Marsh Tit and can easily be confused with it.

The Willow Tit *(Parus montanus)* is the most similar, but has a sooty black cap. It inhabits much of Europe and Asia; in Britain, unlike the former species, it extends as far as the Scottish Highlands, but is also absent from Ireland. The other two species are considerably larger.

The Sombre Tit *(P. lugubris)* has a broad black bib. It inhabits south-east Europe and Asia Minor.

The Siberian Tit *(P. cinctus)* has a dark brown cap. It occurs in northern Scandinavia, in Siberia and in Alaska.

◁ **Blue Tit** · *Parus caeruleus* L. (Further illustration follows p. 91)

Family: Tits (Paridae)

Description: The crown, wings and tail are bright blue; the back is greenish, the underparts yellow with an indistinct grey streak down the breast and belly. The cheeks are white. Young birds resemble the parents. L: $4^1/_2''$, Wt: $^2/_5$ oz.

The song is characterised by a trill at the end and sounds like "zizizizisirrrrr". Soft "sit" calls are also heard, and a scolding phrase like "zeerrettetet". In fact a very wide range of sounds is produced.

Distribution: Europe apart from the extreme north, western Asia and north Africa. In the north Blue Tits are partial migrants while in the south they are mainly resident. Irruptions occur in some years (as with Great Tits)—movements over the Alps, and also into Britain being noted.

Habitat: Similar to the Great Tit's, but does not extend so high into mountain regions.

Breeding: Nests are of typical tit-construction; the Blue Tit uses moss, fine grass, animal hair and wool in sites very similar to the Great Tit's, although smaller holes are often used. Its breeding biology also resembles the Great Tit's. The clutch of seven to fourteen eggs, which look very like Marsh Tits', hatches after 13—16 days' incubation, and the young fly in 19—20 days. Usually single-brooded; second broods seem to be commoner in southern Europe.

Food: Like the Great Tit's, but it takes more spiders.

Allied species:

The Azure Tit *(Parus cyanus)* which is found throughout Russia to east Asia is a species resembling the Blue Tit; it may be told by its white crown, white underparts and greyish-blue upperparts. At migration time it sometimes strays west to central Europe.

Coal Tit · *Parus ater* L. (Illustration follows p. 95, above)

Family: Tits (Paridae)

Description: ♂ and ♀ are alike in colour. The head is glossy black with a conspicuous white patch on the nape, and white cheeks; the back is olive-grey, as are the wings and tail. The wing-coverts are tipped white. The underparts are — apart from a black bib — off-white with a light brown tinge. Juveniles resemble the parents, but the crown is more brownish and lacks gloss; their underparts have a dirty yellow tinge. L: $4^1/_4$″, Wt: *c.* $^1/_3$ oz.

The song "*seecho-seecho-seecho* . . . *chooee-chooee-chooee* . . .", resembles the Great Tit's. Additional notes are a shrill "dee" recalling the Siskin's call-note, soft "sit-sit" calls and (especially when mobbing owls) an explosive "chee" which is often rapidly repeated.

Distribution: Europe, except the extreme north, Asia between 50° and 65° N (also further south in east Asia), and north Africa. In Britain the Coal Tit is well distributed and resident; north European birds are partial migrants.

Habitat: Predominantly pine and fir woods, also mixed woodland; in broad-leaved woodland and parks it is much less common. It is found up to the tree limit in mountain regions.

Blue Tit · *Parus caeruleus* ▷

Breeding: All kinds of small holes serve the Coal Tit as nest sites. Mouse-holes are often used. Its breeding biology is similar to that of other tits.
Food: Like the Great Tit's, but includes more spiders.

Crested Tit · *Parus cristatus* L. (Illustration follows p. 95, below)

Family: Tits (Paridae)
Description: Both sexes are greyish-brown above and off-white, washed pale brown below. There is a black bib while the head bears a crest, pale with dark barring. Juveniles resemble adults. L: $4^1/_2''$, Wt: $^2/_5$ oz.

The Crested Tit's song—a subdued chirping and purring twitter—is seldom heard, but the loud "zizigurr-gurr-gurr" trill is much used. It also makes thin "whispering" calls.

Distribution: Almost all of Europe, but it is lacking from northern Scandinavia and Italy, while in the British Isles it is restricted to an area of north-east Scotland.
Habitat: This is very much a bird of coniferous forest, in which it is found up to the mountain tree limit. But it occurs in mixed woodland too and in southern Europe also in deciduous woods.

Breeding: The Crested Tit is the first of the family to nest in spring, often beginning one or two weeks before the other tits. It generally builds its nest in natural holes. At times it enlarges such holes, especially if they are located in rotten stumps or branches. It accepts nestboxes rather seldom. The general breeding biology resembles that of other tits but only five to eight eggs make up the clutch.
Food: As for other tits: mainly spiders and insects.

◁ **Marsh Tit** · *Parus palustris* (p. 87)

Penduline Tit · *Remiz pendulinus* (L.) (Illustration precedes p. 98)

Family: Penduline tits (Remizidae)
Description: ♂ and ♀ are similar in plumage, although the ♀ is somewhat duller. In breeding plumage the back is reddish-brown, the head greyish-white except for a broad black eye-stripe extending back to the region of the ear, and the underparts cream-coloured with red-brown feathers on the breast. The winter-plumage in general shows less contrast and is more brownish. In young birds the eye-stripe is completely absent, the head is brownish and the back cinnamon. L: 4$^{1}/_{4}$", Wt: $^{1}/_{8}$ oz.

Penduline Tits are adept climbers. Their drawn-out call notes, easily confused with a Reed Bunting's, sound like "seee". The song is a soft twittering.

Distribution: In Europe mainly in the east and in Italy. There are pockets further west, in south Germany, along the Oder, the upper reaches of the Rhone, the Camargue, and the Spanish Mediterranean coast to the mouth of the Guadalquivir. In Asia it occurs approximately between 30° and 55° N. It is a partial migrant, wandering extensively outside the breeding season. There are signs of a westward spread, the first-ever British sighting being reported on the east coast in autumn 1966.
Habitat: Marshy margins of rivers and lakes with willow thickets, swamps with bushy scrub, steppe-forest.

Breeding: The ♂ selects the nesting tree and begins building a nest on a suitable branch, singing vigorously. If after some time no ♀ has joined him, he starts another nest somewhere else. When a ♀ appears, the structure is completed with her energetic help. The nest is fixed right at the end of a twig so that it hangs down like a flask (in some areas nests are built in reeds). A short tunnel-like entry is left open.

Coal Tit · *Parus ater* (p. 91) Above ▷

Crested Tit · *Parus cristatus* Below ▷

Grass stems and a great deal of animal and vegetable down are the materials used. The ♀ lays five to eight pure white eggs. During the incubation period the pair-bond is often relaxed and the ♂ mates with a second (sometimes even with a third) ♀, with which another brood is begun. The ♂ takes no share in the actual nest duties. The eggs are hatched in 12—15 days, and the young leave the nest after 15—20 days. After the breeding season Penduline Tits move about in small parties.

Food: In swampy areas insects and spiders at all stages of development, in winter also small seeds of the reed and other marsh plants.

Long-tailed Tit · *Aegithalos caudatus* (L.) (Illustration follows p. 99)

Family: Long-tailed tits (Aegithalidae)

Description: Both sexes are largely blackish above, with vinous feathers on the shoulders, and predominantly white below; on each side of the white head is a more or less well-defined black stripe which joins the black back (some northern birds lack these). The very long tail makes this otherwise tiny bird unmistakable. Juveniles resemble adults. L: 5¹/₂″ (of which 2″ are tail), Wt: a little under ¹/₃ oz.

Outside the breeding season Long-tailed Tits keep in parties, moving in short flights from tree to tree, and feeding acrobatically among the twigs like other tits. They call constantly, mainly with a thin "sisisi", also "tcherr". The song is a weak, rapid tinkling.

Distribution: Europe apart from the extreme north, western Asia, west Persia, and large areas further east in Asia below 60° N. British birds are resident, but northern continental populations move south in winter.

Habitat: Mixed and broad-leaved woodland, parkland, orchards and thick timbered hedges. Rarely above 3,000 ft in mountain country.

Breeding: In late winter the flocks break up and pairs are formed. The nest is oval or egg-shaped, of moss, plant-down, cobwebs, etc.,

◁ **Penduline Tit** · *Remiz pendulinus* (p. 95)

decorated with lichens and bits of bark and thickly lined with feathers and wool. The entrance is near the top. It is often well hidden or blended with the site, which may be high in a tree-fork or among conifer needles, quite low down among creepers or in a thorny bush. Both partners take part in building. The clutch consists of eight to thirteen eggs, white with light red speckles. Incubation is by the ♀ alone, and lasts 12—14 days. The young fly when about 15 days old and remain with the parents long afterwards. Generally single-brooded. *Food:* Small insects in all developmental stages and spiders. Mostly insect eggs and pupae in winter.

Bearded Tit · *Panurus biarmicus* (L.) (Illustration follows p. 103)

Family: Babblers (Timaliidae)
Description: The upperparts and tail are cinnamon, primaries pale grey to whitish, underparts reddish-grey. The ♂ has an ash-grey head with broad black moustachial stripes; its under tail-coverts are deep black. The ♀ has a brownish head without moustachial stripes. Young birds are like the ♀, but have very dark backs. L: 6¹/₄″.

Bearded Tits' calls, often heard as the birds move unseen among the reeds, are a nasal "ping-ping", a sharp "ziss" and a wheezing "chirr". The song is a soft twittering into which these call-notes are woven.

Distribution: The main strongholds are south Russia, Asia Minor and eastern Europe (East Prussia, Lower Austria, Hungary, eastern Greece, the Danube delta, Crimea); further west there are isolated pockets in the Po delta, south Italy and Sicily, the Camargue, eastern Spain (coastal and inland), west France, Holland and England. In England it only breeds in the south-east, in a few areas near the coast. When the population is high, many birds move out in autumn and may cover long distances. In 1965 numbers of both Dutch and British-bred birds wandered west on an unusual scale and were recorded in many English counties.
Habitat: Extensive reed-beds by lakes and in marshes.

Long-tailed Tit · *Aegithalos caudatus* ▷

Breeding: The nest is built by both partners. It is never suspended between reed stems, but is placed low down on a base of broken dead reeds. It is made of reed flowers and grass stems and is lined with fine stems and often feathers. Sometimes a kind of screen is built above the nest. The four to seven eggs have a whitish ground and blackish-brown speckles and streaks. Both ♂ and ♀ sit; incubation takes 11—13 days and fledging barely two weeks. Two broods, and perhaps three at times, are reared in a season.

Food: Small insects in all stages of development, in winter also seeds such as those of reed and reedmace.

Nuthatch · *Sitta europaea* L. (Illustration precedes p. 106)

Family: Nuthatches (Sittidae)

Description: The upperparts are blue-grey, underparts buffish, becoming paler towards the throat. On each side a black streak runs from the bill through the eye to the back of the head. The outer tips of the tail are whitish. The flanks of the ♂ are chestnut, those of the ♀ duller brown. Juveniles resemble the ♀. L: 5½″, Wt: *c.* ⅘ oz.

Nuthatches are very vocal. The most striking call is a metallic "tui-tuit-tuit . . .". The song is a whistling "twee-twee-twee", and a trilling "treerrr" is also frequently heard, as is a thin preliminary "tsit". Nuthatches are expert climbers, and can even run head-first down tree-trunks and branches.

Distribution: Europe (including England and Wales but not Scotland or Ireland) to about 60° N, southwest Asia, the Himalayas and Asia between latitudes 50° and 65°. In east Asia it is found from Amur to India. It is a resident and wanders very little.

Habitat: Deciduous, mixed and coniferous woods with mature timber, parks and orchards where there are old trees, extending to the tree limit in mountain areas.

Breeding: Nuthatches breed in holes in trees, also in nestboxes and even holes in walls. Before the breeding season begins a previous year's hole may be largely cleared of material. The nest consists mainly of flakes of pine-tree bark; should this not be available, the birds use dead leaves and bits of bark from other trees for building. The parents reduce the size of the entrance hole with clay or mud until it is only just wide enough to admit them. The four to eight eggs, white with red spotting, are brooded only by the ♀, which is fed during this time by the ♂. Incubation takes 15—18 days, and fledging 24 days. Normally single-brooded.

Food: Smaller insects, their larvae and pupae, spiders, seeds (especially oil-rich ones in winter), animal and vegetable fat. The Nuthatch likes to visit bird tables in winter, where its favourite choice is sunflower seeds. Many of these are taken off and hidden.

Allied species:
The Rock Nuthatch *(Sitta neumayer)*, found in south-east Europe and south-west Asia, resembles our Nuthatch but is paler below. It plasters up large nest-cavities with an entrance funnel in clefts in cliffs.
The small Corsican Nuthatch *(S. whiteheadi)*, with black crown and white stripe above the eye, breeds in tree-holes in the mountain forests of Corsica.

Wallcreeper · *Tichodroma muraria* (L.) (Illustration follows p. 107)

Family: Nuthatches (Sittidae) *Subfamily:* Wallcreepers (Tichodromadinae)
Description: Above, both sexes are predominantly ash-grey; the tail and flight feathers are largely blackish, the underside is dark grey. There are two rows of white spots on the primaries, while the carpal feathers, wing-coverts and lower parts of the primaries and secondaries are bright carmine-red. In both sexes the throat is black in breeding plumage, and greyish-white outside the breeding season. Juveniles are like adults in winter plumage. L: 6¼".
The Wallcreeper attracts attention through its butterfly-like flight. Its calls are piping and sound like "tieu". The song consists of a melodious sequence of piping calls and may be rendered "sisisiseui".

Bearded Tit · *Panurus biarmicus* (p. 99) ♂ ▷

The Wallcreeper often sings while climbing—progressing up rock walls in a series of hops using its wings to help it. This results in constant wing-flicking, and produces a flashing effect from the red feathers and white spots.

Distribution: The mountain massifs of Europe: the Pyrenees, Alps and Apenines, the Balkan peninsula and the Carpathians, also the Tatra. It has also been found in the Sierra Nevada. Outside Europe it occurs in the mountains of southern Asia Minor, Persia and from the Himalayas to west China. It may also breed in the Atlas region in north Africa. It is a resident which does not move about much outside the breeding season, merely spreading onto lower ground in winter.
Habitat: Rocky parts of higher mountains.

Breeding: Wallcreepers prefer to place their nests in the walls of steep rocky gullies with mountain streams rushing through them. But nests may also be found in crevices in cliffs, sometimes even in holes in walls. They are built of moss, lichens and bents and are occasionally also lined with feathers. The four or five eggs have red-brown spotting on a white ground. The incubation period is 18—19 days and the young fly after about 26 days. Single-brooded.
Food: Insects and spiders taken from cracks and fissures in cliffs and walls. Flying insects are also taken.

Treecreeper · *Certhia familiaris* L. (Illustration precedes p. 110)

Family: Treecreepers (Certhiidae)
Description: ♂ and ♀ are brown above with whitish and blackish streaks on the head and upper back. The underparts are almost pure white. Juveniles resemble the parents. L: 5″, Wt: *c.* 1/3 oz.

The most noticeable call is a high-pitched "sree", often given several times in succession. The song, a twittering with a final trill, is a bit reminiscent of Blue Tit and Wren, but is much softer.

◁ **Nuthatch** · *Sitta europaea* (p. 102)

Distribution: The British Isles, the Pyrenees, the French Massif Central, nearly all Europe above 40° N apart from northern Scandinavia, the mountains of west and central Asia, the area from the Urals to Japan below 60° N; North America, from the south-west coast of Alaska to the centre of the continent and south of latitude 55° to the east coast. Mainly resident. The American population is often regarded as forming a distinct species *(Certhia americana)*.

Habitat: This is a woodland bird, on the Continent found mainly at higher altitudes up to the tree limit, sometimes coming down to lower more open ground in winter. In Britain it occurs at all heights, and breeds in well-timbered park- and farmland as well as in woods.

Breeding: The nest is sited behind loose bark, cracks in tree trunks or stumps, woodpiles, nestboxes, even suitable cracks in sheds. It is formed with fine twigs, moss and chips of wood and lined with fine bark strips, wool and sometimes feathers. The four to seven white eggs have reddish spots. They hatch in 15 days and the young fly after 16—17 days. One or two broods a year.

Food: Small insects in all stages of development, and spiders; in winter occasionally conifer seeds, bits of moss and algae.

Allied species:
The Short-toed Treecreeper *(Certhia brachydactula)* occurs on low ground in central Europe, and generally in southern Europe and north Africa. It is distinguished from the Treecreeper by off-white underparts with brownish-washed flanks. Its song "tit-didelit-dit" sounds as if it is cut short. Hard "tit" calls may also be heard. It inhabits chiefly gardens, parks and lowland forest, and locally cork-oak woods in southern Europe.

Wren · *Troglodytes troglodytes* (L.) (Illustration follows p. 111)

Family: Wrens (Troglodytidae)
Description: Both sexes are brownish above, with faint barring on

Wallcreeper · *Tichodroma muraria* (p. 103) ▷

wings and tail. The underside is a pale dirty grey-brown with darker longitudinal bars on the flanks. There is a light stripe above the eye. Juveniles are similar to adults. L: just over 3″, Wt: *c.* ⅓ oz.

The Wren always seems excited; it darts about like a mouse, its tail cocked up when it perches. Its movements are accompanied by a hard "tettettetet" which alters to a churring "zerrrr" when very agitated. The song, an alternation of tuneful metallic notes and trills, sounds surprisingly loud; it is usually given from a raised perch.

Distribution: Europe, save for the extreme north, north Africa, south-west, central and east Asia between latitudes 25—55° N; North America, from the south-west tip of Alaska—roughly between 35° and 60° N—to Labrador. The Wren is predominantly resident.
Habitat: Woods of all kinds, damp valleys with scrub, parks and gardens with plenty of bushes and low cover. It has even adapted itself to living on some remote treeless Scottish islands.

Breeding: The ♂ builds a number of externally complete "cock's nests" of which one is lined and laid in by the ♀. It is a domed structure, firmly made of moss, leaves, grasses, etc., lined with feathers. The nest, with its entrance at the side, is usually well hidden among tree-roots, under overhanging banks, holes in walls, under bridges, sometimes also in nestboxes, in ivy, thorn scrub, or among dense shoots, usually at no great height. The five to eight white eggs with red speckles are incubated by the ♀ for 14—16 days. The young leave after 15—18 days. Generally double-brooded.
Food: Small insects at all developmental stages and spiders; sometimes small seeds in winter.

Dipper · *Cinclus cinclus* (L.) (Illustration precedes p. 114)

Family: Dippers (Cinclidae)
Description: The sexes look alike. The head is grey-brown; back, wings and tail are slate-grey. A white "bib" covers throat and breast; it is

◁ **Treecreeper** · *Certhia familiaris* (p. 106)

sharply demarcated by a zone of chestnut, which gradually merges into dark grey. Juveniles are slate grey above with dark feather-edges, their underparts from throat to belly yellowish-white washed with grey. L: 7″, Wt: *c.* 2 oz.

When disturbed by one's approach Dippers often give their "zerrb" alarm call. The song, given by both sexes, is a twittering and sometimes grating warble.

Distribution: Almost all of Europe, western Asia, the Urals and various central Asian mountain ranges. The Dipper is a resident.
Habitat: Swift-running streams; it avoids strongly polluted water.

Breeding: Territories usually extend ³/₄—1¹/₄ miles along watercourses. For preference nests are lodged in crevices in stream-banks, also often beneath bridges. The nest is spherical with a side-entrance, of moss and grass, frequently lined with leaves; it is built almost entirely by the ♀. In some cases the nest just fits into a cavity and little material apart from the cup is needed. By contrast nests on projecting rocks or girders of bridges tend to be bulky and resemble outsize wrens' nests. Dippers often use the same nest or site for many years. The four to six pure white eggs are incubated by the ♀ alone, for 14—18 days. The young leave when about 20 days old (but earlier if disturbed). Often double-brooded.
Food: Chiefly larvae of water insects, and water fleas *(Gammarus)* caught in shallow water. Dippers can also swim under water (using their wings) and feed on the bottom. Recent studies have shown that they only exceptionally take small fish.

Mistle Thrush · *Turdus viscivorus* L. (Illustration follows p. 115)

Family: Thrushes, etc. (Muscicapidae) *Subfamily:* Thrushes (Turdinae)
Description: In both sexes the upperparts are mainly grey-brown with some areas tinged dusty-grey. The outer tail feathers have white tips to their outer webs. The underparts are whitish with relatively large

Wren · *Troglodytes troglodytes* (p. 107) ▷

blackish-brown spots. The under wing-coverts are white. Juveniles resemble adults but are paler in colour and spotted above. L: 10¹/₂", Wt: *c.* 4¹/₂ oz.

The song consists of short hurried phrases, flute-like, far-carrying and fairly even in pitch. It suggests a series of fanfares, and is quite characteristic, as is the loud, harsh "cherr" call-note.

Distribution: Europe, except for western and northern Scandinavia, large areas of Asia up to 100° E, north Africa. The Mistle Thrush is a partial migrant, northern birds moving to warmer areas in winter.
Habitat: Predominantly woodland, with a preference for open woods; up to the tree limit on mountains. In some areas (including Britain) parks, orchards and gardens are also favoured.

Breeding: The usual nest site is in a tree-fork at some height from the ground, or next to the trunk of a conifer (often in the crown), infrequently low down. The nest is made from grass stems, moss and twigs, and in contrast to the Blackbird's nest contains hardly any mud. The three to five eggs have a pale bluish-green ground with irregular reddish-brown spotting and are incubated only by the ♀. They hatch in 12—15 days and the young fly when 13—15 days old. Probably quite often double-brooded if the first attempt is successful.
Food: Insects and their larvae, worms, snails, spiders, berries and fallen fruit, mistletoe berries in winter.
This species feeds chiefly on the ground, where it often tears the surface open with its bill.

Fieldfare · *Turdus pilaris* L. (Illustration precedes p. 118)

Family: Thrushes, etc. (Muscicapidae) *Subfamily:* Thrushes (Turdinae)
Description: ♂ and ♀ are similar in colour, the ♀ being slightly paler. The head and rump are grey, the back reddish-brown. The belly is white, while the rest of the underparts have a diffuse pale rusty ground colour with dense blackish spotting. In juvenile plumage the colours

◁ **Dipper** · *Cinclus cinclus* (p. 110)

show less contrast and the grey head and rump are washed brownish. L: 9³/₄—10¹/₄″, Wt: *c.* 3¹/₂ oz.

The usual calls are a loud "chack chack" and a soft "zeeh". The song, a weak twittering and wheezing, is usually delivered in flight.

Distribution: Europe and Asia, chiefly between latitudes 50° and 70° N, and between longitudes 5° and 135° E. The Fieldfare has also colonised the southern tip of Greenland. In recent years there has been a westward, and especially south-westward, spread; the middle reaches of the Rhine and the upper Rhône valley form the present western limits of breeding. The species is a partial migrant, often moving south or west in autumn. Large numbers spend the winter in the British Isles (very recently a few have nested in north Scotland).
Habitat: In various parts of their range Fieldfares breed in natural forests and woodland edge, parkland, orchards, well-timbered farmland, sometimes gardens; up to 5,500 ft above sea-level.

Breeding: Where the bird is common, several nests are usually found near each other and are defended communally against predators. The nest resembles the Blackbird's, and like it contains much earth. It is usually sited in the fork of a branch, or close against a trunk. The four to seven eggs, fairly densely spotted with reddish-brown on a greenish-blue ground, are incubated by the ♀ alone. They hatch in 13—14 days and the young fly after 14 days. Often double-brooded.
Food: Insects, spiders, worms and snails, also berries and fruit. On parts of the Continent fruit crops may be damaged in late summer, but by the time they reach Britain there are usually only windfalls available, on which they feed freely. Winter flocks often feed on open farmland.

Song Thrush · *Turdus philomelos* Brehm (Illustration follows p. 119)

Family: Thrushes, etc. (Muscicapidae) *Subfamily:* Thrushes (Turdinae)
Description: Both sexes have brown upperparts, wings and tail. The

Mistle Thrush · *Turdus viscivorus* (p. 111) ▷

underparts are whitish, while the breast is tinged creamy and has dark brown spots. The under wing-coverts are pale brown. Young birds are like the parents, apart from some buff streaking above. L: 9″, Wt: c. 2¹/₂ oz.

When taking wing and in flight, Song Thrushes often give a soft "sip" call. If highly alarmed they rap out a rapid "tickticktick...". The song consists of fluting and whistling phrases, repeated several times in varying sequence, interspersed with harder phrases, often rendered as "pretty dick-pretty dick".

Distribution: Europe, except the extreme north, south to latitude 42°, the mountains of northern Asia Minor to the Caspian Sea, between 50° and 65° N and east to about 110° E. The Song Thrush is a partial migrant, many birds from northerly regions moving south or west to milder areas for the winter.

Habitat: All kinds of woodland, parks, farmland, orchards, also in parts of its range (as in Britain) gardens; up to the tree limit in mountain regions.

Breeding: Most of the nests found are in bushes or hedges between 2 and 10 ft above the ground, but in woodland many are built in trees at heights up to 25 ft or more, and some are actually on the ground. The nest of grass, moss, leaves, etc. has a smooth inner lining of mud or soft wood pulp. Usually three to five eggs are laid, sky-blue with a few black spots mainly at the blunt end. Incubation is by the ♀ only and takes 12—14 days, rarely longer. The young usually leave the nest when 13—14 days old. Two broods annually as a rule, sometimes more.

Food: Predominantly earthworms, followed by snails, whose shells are broken by battering against stones—so-called "thrushes' anvils"—also insects and, in autumn, berries and fruit.

◁ **Fieldfare** · *Turdus pilaris* (p. 114)

Ring Ouzel · *Turdus torquatus* L. (Illustration precedes p. 122, above)

Familiy: Thrushes, etc. (Muscicapidae) *Subfamily:* Thrushes (Turdinae)
Description: The ♂ is predominantly black with faint pale edgings to the body feathers. The white crescent-shaped band across its breast makes it unmistakable. The ♀ is browner, with an off-white breastband. Juveniles resemble the ♀ but are paler below with darker brown spotting. L: 9½″, Wt: *c.* 4 oz.

The song is somewhat reminiscent of that of the Song Thrush, but sounds wilder and less pure; it also has a much smaller range of variation. A chuckling phrase sounding like "tru-tru-tru" may often be heard; it is characteristic of this species. When agitated the Ring Ouzel utters a hard "tack-tack-tack".

Distribution: The higher hills and mountains of the British Isles and Scandinavia, the Pyrenees, Vosges, Black Forest, Alps, the mountains of Bavaria and western and northern Czechoslovakia, the Carpathians, Balkans, Caucasus, Elbrus and Transcaspian mountains. The species is a partial migrant, wintering in southern Europe. (The British stock is entirely migratory.)
Habitat: The Ring Ouzel is a bird of high ground, breeding usually from about 1,000 ft above sea-level upwards in Britain, but rarely below 3,000 ft on the Continent. There it chiefly inhabits open conifer woods, whereas British birds usually live on open moorland, favouring gullies in particular.

Breeding: A characteristic thrush-type nest is built with a lining of grass. In Britain it is very often on a bank more or less concealed by overhanging heather or grass, or on a rock ledge, and often near a stream; nests a few feet up in a tree are not common here, whereas in parts of Europe this is the usual site. The three to six eggs, greenish-white flecked reddish-brown, are incubated only by the ♀ for 12—14 days. The young fly when about two weeks old. Often double-brooded.
Food: Much as for other thrushes, worms forming the principal item.

Song Trush · *Turdus philomelos* (p. 115) ▷

◁ **Ring Ouzel** · *Turdus torquatus* (p. 119) ♀ Above

◁ **Redwing** · *Turdus iliacus* L. Below

Family: Thrushes, etc. (Muscicapidae) *Subfamily:* Thrushes (Turdinae)
Description: The sexes look alike, both being a bit darker brown above than the Song Thrush. There is a whitish stripe over the eye and another marks the lower margin of the cheek. The underparts are whitish with blackish-brown streaks. The flanks and under wing-coverts are rust-red. Juveniles are like the parents though more heavily streaked, and are paler red on the flanks. L: $8^{1}/_{4}''$, Wt: *c.* 2 oz.

The song is given from a high perch and consists of four or five fluty notes sounding like "tree", and a subdued babbling. The frequently used call is a soft drawn-out "seee"; it is often heard from migrants at night.

Distribution: Scandinavia, Iceland, north-east Europe and Asia above 55° N, as far as Siberia. Redwings migrate to winter-quarters in western Europe; they are common winter visitors to Britain, often being seen in flocks. Small but increasing numbers now breed in northern Scotland.
Habitat: Woodland and parks; farmland in winter.

Breeding: The nest is a typical thrush affair, with a grass lining. It is usually low in a tree or bush, or often on the ground. The four to six eggs have a greenish-white ground with brownish spots. The breeding biology is similar to the Song Thrush's.
Food: Like that of the Song Thrush. In autumn and winter hawthorn berries are much favoured if available.

Blackbird · *Turdus merula* L. (Illustration follows p. 123, above)

Family: Thrushes, etc. (Muscicapidae) *Subfamily:* Thrushes (Turdinae)
Description: The ♂ is completely black, with faint gloss. Its bill is orange-yellow. The ♀ is for the most part dark brown, the throat being paler with blackish markings, and the bill horn-coloured. Young

birds are like the ♀ but have paler underparts, distinctly spotted with darker brown. L: 10″, Wt: *c.* 3¹/₂ oz.

Far-carrying, fluting phrases interpersed with short shrill notes, constitute the Blackbird's varied and beautiful song. Calls include a piercing "dix-dix-dix" (used at roosting-time and when mobbing owls), a shrill warning chatter, and a high "seee" and a "chook-chook" which denote different degrees of agitation. It is one of the earliest and latest singers of the day, singing from tree-tops and roof-ridges.

Distribution: Europe except northern Scandinavia, north Africa, Asia Minor, Palestine, Syria, north Persia, and from the Transcaspian range—roughly between latitudes 20° and 40° N—as far as China. The Blackbird is a partial migrant. Many north European birds winter in Britain, whereas the majority of British-bred birds stay put, although some do move to Ireland or France.
Habitat: The Blackbird must originally have been an inhabitant of woodland of various types. Nowadays it is also common on farmland, in parks, gardens and even city squares.

Breeding: The breeding biology is generally similar to that of other thrushes. A lot of mud is used in making the nest-cup, but there is an inner layer of grass. Only the ♀ incubates the three to six eggs, which are greenish with reddish-brown flecking. They hatch in 11—14 days and fledging takes about 13 days. Two or three broods annually.
Food: As for other thrushes. Many caterpillars are fed to nestlings in woodland in May and June.

Allied species:
The Black-throated Thrush *(Turdus atrogularis)* has penetrated from Asia into north-east Europe.

Blackbird · *Turdus merula* ♂ Above ▷

Black Wheatear · *Oenanthe leucura* (Gmel.), ♂ Below ▷

Family: Thrushes etc. (Muscicapidae) *Subfamily:* Thrushes (Turdinae)
Description: The ♂ is uniformly black with white rump, upper and

under tail-coverts and sides to the tail. The ♀ is like the ♂, only more brownish. Juveniles are dull black with the same white markings. L: 7″, Wt: *c.* 1½ oz.

On the ground it attracts attention by its habit of fanning its raised tail, and by its whinnying calls. The song is made up of musical and scratchy phrases. A harsh "chack", a nasal "teet" and a shrill "kreerr" are used when agitated.

Distribution: The Iberian peninsula, the mountains between Marseilles and Genoa, north Africa. The species is resident.
Habitat: Wild mountain ravines, extensive boulder-fields and rocky wastes.

Breeding: The commonest nest site is in a rock-fissure. The foundations are built largely by the ♂, but also by the ♀, of flat stones. A little wall is often formed at the entrance. The nest proper is of dry grass stems lined with feathers and hair. The four or five bluish-white eggs with reddish-grey spots are incubated entirely by the ♀ for about 16 days. The young leave the nest at about 15 days. Thereafter the family stays in a loose group until winter. Normally single-brooded.
Food: Insects of all sorts, especially grasshoppers; also spiders and small lizards, various berries in autumn.

◁ **Wheatear** · *Oenanthe oenanthe* (L.), ♀

Family: Thrushes etc. (Muscicapidae) *Subfamily:* Thrushes (Turdinae)
Description: The ♂ in breeding plumage has the head, nape and back grey, and the rump, upper tail-coverts and upper part of the outer tail feathers white. The rest of the tail and the wings are black. The forehead is white, and a black stripe runs from the base of the bill through the eye to the ear-coverts. Above this lies a white stripe. The underparts are cream-coloured. The ♀ is brownish above, with darker ear-coverts, brownish-cream below. The rump and tail are coloured as in the ♂. In winter plumage the ♂ resembles the ♀. Juveniles are obscurely spotted greyish-brown above and below; their rump and tail

pattern is like the adults'. Wheatears "bob" or "curtsy" when excited. L: 6″, Wt: 1 oz.

The hasty song consists of short, mainly rather lark-like phrases. "Tac-tac" calls and a high "weet" indicate alarm.

Distribution: Europe, the greater part of Asia, south to about 35° N, Iceland, the coast of Greenland and north-east America between 50° and 80° N, large areas in Alaska. A summer visitor, the Wheatear winters principally in the savannah areas of Africa.
Habitat: Mainly open stony country; in Britain (and many other parts of its range) hill moorland and treeless coastal islands are favoured; in parts of Europe the bird frequents terraced vineyards.

Breeding: The ♂ shows various possible breeding holes in the ground or in stone walls to the ♀, which makes the final choice. The nest is made of dry bents lined with hair and feathers. The four to seven eggs are pale blue with a few faint reddish or grey-brown freckles. They are incubated by the ♀ only, for 13—16 days. The young leave the nest when 14—16 days old. Often single-brooded, but two broods are regular in some areas.
Food: All kinds of insects, spiders, small worms, snails. Wheatears have also been seen eating berries.

Allied species:
The Black-eared Wheatear *(Oenanthe hispanica)* inhabits southern Europe. It is sandy and white in colour with either a black throat or in other cases just a black "bridle" and black wings. When agitated it flicks both wings sideways.
The Pied Wheatear *(O. pleschanka)* is found in Rumania, southern Russia and the Crimea. It has a grey-white crown and nape, black back and wings, its throat and breast are also black, while the belly is whitish. The ♀♀ are much like ♀ Wheatears.
The Isabelline Wheatear *(O. isabellina)* breeds in European Turkey and occurs on migration around the Aegean; it resembles the ♀ Wheatear but is paler and larger.

Stonechat · *Saxicola torquata* L., ♂ ▷

Family: Thrushes etc. (Muscicapidae) *Subfamily:* Thrushes (Turdinae)

Description: The ♂ has a black head and throat with white on the sides of the neck, and a rusty-red breast. Its back is dark brown with darker streaks, as are the wings apart from a narrow white bar. The rump is whitish, the tail dark brown. The ♀ is more brownish, less brightly marked. Juvenile plumage is mainly paler, with darker brown mottling. L: 5″, Wt: *c.* ½ oz.

The Stonechat likes exposed perches such as the tops of bushes or boulders, and telephone wires. The alarm call when agitated is a sharp "weet-tac-tac". Short phrases containing a mixture of scratchy and musical notes make up the song.

Distribution: Europe, except the north-east and Scandinavia, Asia Minor, also large stretches of Asia as far as Japan, north, east, south and a part of west Africa. It is a partial migrant, many birds wintering in western Europe and the Mediterranean region.
Habitat: The Stonechat prefers heathland and open stony ground with scattered bushes (particularly gorse). Most British birds breed on suitable stretches of the coast. On parts of the Continent the bird also occurs in vineyards and meadowland.

Breeding: The nest is well hidden on the ground among gorse or grass tussocks, sometimes (abroad) in a depression under stones. It consists of dry bents and a hair or wool lining. The four to six eggs are bluish-green with fine reddish-brown speckles. Only the ♀ sits, incubation taking 14—15 days and fledging about two weeks, although the young will leave the nest earlier if disturbed. Normally double-brooded, but three broods in a season are quite frequent, and even four have been recorded.
Food: Smaller insects of all kinds and their larvae, also spiders.

◁ **Whinchat** · *Saxicola rubetra* (L.), ♂

Family: Thrushes etc. (Muscicapidae) *Subfamily:* Thrushes (Turdinae)
Description: The ♂ is brown above with dark streaking. The upper half of its outer tail feathers are white, the remainder brown. It has dark brown cheeks and a white stripe over the eye. Its underparts are creamy,

with the breast suffused reddish-brown. The ♀ is similar in plumage, but the colours are less bright and contrasting. Juveniles resemble the ♀ but have light and dark mottling on both upper- and underparts. L: 5¼″, Wt: ²/₃ oz.

The song, formed of short, mostly "scratchy" phrases, rather resembles the Stonechat's. It is delivered from the top of a bush, fence-post or from telephone wires. A "wee-tick-tick" call is often used.

Distribution: Europe, except the extreme south and north, a region of the central Russian steppes, the Caucasus and the Transcaspian region. It is a summer visitor, and winters in tropical Africa.
Habitat: Rough meadows or waste ground and moors (often damp), also chalk downs, where there are bushes or posts for perches.

Breeding: The nest is well hidden among ground-vegetation (lower illustration preceding p. 238, below). The 4—7 eggs are incubated by the ♀ alone, for 14 days. The young leave the nest when about 2 weeks old. Mostly single-brooded.
Food: Small insects and their larvae, spiders.

Blue Rock Thrush · *Monticola solitarius* (L.), ♂ in winter plumage. Above ▷

Family: Thrushes etc. (Muscicapidae) *Subfamily:* Thrushes (Turdinae)
Description: The ♂ is mostly bluish-grey, the head actually becoming sky-blue in worn plumage. Grey or grey-brown feather-tips usually make the breast look scaly. The ♀ is more greyish-brown, with bluish gloss above. Her underparts are barred with lighter and darker brown, while her throat is tinged rusty-brown. Juveniles are like the ♀. L: 8″, Wt: *c.* 2½ oz.

The melancholy song—of short flute-like phrases mixed with scratchy notes—is given from an exposed perch or in pipit-like song-flight. When alarmed it makes a snarling "chrrackrr", while a plaintive "yeep" denotes excitement. It "bobs" like a Wheatear.

Black Redstart · *Phoenicurus ochruros* (p. 134) ♀ Below ▷

Distribution: Southern Europe from the Iberian peninsula to the Bosphorus, north Africa, Asia Minor, Persia, the Hindu Kush, the Himalayas, eastern Asia to Japan and the Philippines. In the western Mediterranean region the Blue Rock Thrush is largely resident, in north-east Greece it is a partial migrant.

Habitat: Precipitous crags, steep-walled ravines, quarries and ruins in stony sparsely vegetated country, sometimes also coastal cliffs.

Breeding: Nests are sited in rock-crannies and holes in walls, often right in caves or cellars of ruins. They are loosely built of twigs and dry grasses. The three to five eggs have a pale bluish-green ground with occasional pale red spots which are only noticed on careful examination. The ♀ alone sits, incubation taking about 14 days. The young leave the nest when rather over two weeks old and hide from danger in holes in the rocks. Only one brood per year, although replacement nests are common. After the breeding season ♂ and ♀ often occupy their own "feeding territories" which they defend by vigorous song against others of their species.

Food: The Blue Rock Thrush has similar feeding habits to a Wheatear or Redstart, taking insects (especially grasshoppers), spiders, centipedes, lizards and small snakes.

Allied species:
The Rock Thrush *(Monticola saxatilis),* resembles the Blue Rock Thrush in its habits and occupies similar habitats, although mostly at higher altitudes. It differs from the latter in having a rust-red breast and tail. The head and upper back are blue-grey, while there is a white patch on the lower back. In winter plumage the ♂ resembles the ♀. The ♀ is reddish-grey with darker mottling and has a rust-coloured tail.

Black Redstart · *Phoenicurus ochruros* (Gmel.)(Illustration follows p. 131)

Family: Thrushes etc. (Muscicapidae) *Subfamily:* Thrushes (Turdinae)
Description: The ♂ is grey-black with a black throat and a white flash

◁ **Redstart** · *Phoenicurus phoenicurus* ♂

on the wings. The tail, apart from the central feathers, is rusty-red. The ♀ is smoky- to slate-grey with rust-red tail. Younger ♂ ♂ are rather like the ♀, as are juveniles, although the latter have a more scaly appearance. L: 5¹/₂″, Wt: *c.* ³/₅ oz.

Black Redstarts like exposed perches where they advertise their presence by bowing and tail-shivering. When agitated they use a metallic "hit-teck-teck"; the song goes something like "didididit-tchrch-dididididit".

Distribution: Europe (but in Britain only a few pairs breed, in the south, while in Scandinavia the species is confined to south Sweden), north Africa, Asia Minor, high ground from the Caucasus to the Himalayas and as far as western China. It is a partial migrant, wintering in western Europe and the Mediterranean area.
Habitat: The Black Redstart was originally a bird of cliffs, which it still is to a large extent in south Europe. It has become adapted to human habitations, breeding in buildings and ruins.

Breeding: The nest is built, like the Blue Rock Thrush's, in crevices in rocks or walls, sometimes also inside caves. It consists of dead grass and moss lined with hairs and feathers. The ♀ alone incubates the four to six pure white eggs, for about 14 days. The fledging period is about 16 days. Normally double-brooded.
Food: Mainly insects, spiders and insect larvae; many berries (especially elderberries) are taken in autumn.

Redstart · *Phoenicurus phoenicurus* (L.) (Illustration precedes p. 134)

Family: Thrushes etc. (Muscicapidae) *Subfamily:* Thrushes (Turdinae)
Description: The ♂ is ashy-grey above, with a white forehead. Its tail is red with brown central feathers, the throat and cheeks are black and the breast rusty-red. The ♀ is greyish-brown above with a red tail, reddish-grey beneath. Juveniles have obscure light and dark mottling both on the upperparts and underparts. L: 5¹/₂″, Wt: *c.* ¹/₂ oz.

Robin · *Erithacus rubecula* (p. 138) ▷

In its actions and many of its calls it resembles the Black Redstart. The song is variable, usually starting with short whistling notes followed by one or more short trills.

Distribution: Europe except north-east Scandinavia and some southern regions, north Africa, Asia Minor, the Crimea, the Caucasus, parts of Asia between 50° and about 65° N as far as 110° E. It is a summer visitor which winters from Arabia and east Africa westwards to northern west Africa, also to some extent in the Mediterranean area.

Habitat: Open woodland and woodland edge, also (especially on the Continent) parks, orchards and gardens. In Britain it is commonest in woods of oak, birch and Scots pine; it is also found in England near slow-flowing rivers with pollard willows.

Breeding: The Redstart is a hole-nester, using holes in trees and in stone walls, short tunnels along the ground under dead bracken, and often nestboxes; the nest resembles a Black Redstart's. The hole is chosen by the ♂, which "advertises" it to the ♀ by singing from the entrance, repeatedly showing its white forehead from within or fluttering outside with bright red tail fanned. The three to nine (generally five to seven) eggs are light blue and unmarked. The breeding biology resembles the Black Redstart's, but the present species is usually single-brooded.

Food: On the whole very like the Black Redstart's.

Allied species:
The Red-flanked Bluetail *(Tarsiger cyanurus)* breeds in north-east Europe and further east.

◁ **Robin** · *Erithacus rubecula* (L.)

Family: Thrushes etc. (Muscicapidae) *Subfamily:* Thrushes (Turdinae)
Description: Both ♂ and ♀ have olive-brown upperparts and the forehead, cheeks, throat and breast orange- to rusty-red; the belly is whitish. Juveniles have light and dark spotting above and below, and no red on the breast. L: 5¹/₂", Wt: *c.* ³/₅ oz.

The Robin is familiar to all as it hops perkily about on the ground with frequent sudden pauses, when it often "curtsies". Continental birds are often very shy. The song, made up of high warbling notes, interspersed with shriller phrases, is usually delivered from a raised perch or from cover. It is characterised by its "soft" tone and the somewhat melancholy nature of the very varied phrases. The scolding "ticking" and a high drawn-out "seee" are frequently-heard notes.

Distribution: Europe except for northern Scandinavia and some stretches of the Mediterranean coasts of France and Spain, also north Africa, Asia Minor, the Caucasus, north Persia and western Russia. The Robin is a partial migrant, birds from colder areas moving to western Europe and the Mediterranean area for the winter.

Habitat: All kinds of woods, especially damp and low-lying ones, parks, gardens and farmland with hedgerows. Territories with a tall layer of deciduous vegetation and mossy ground-cover are preferred. In the southern part of its range the Robin inhabits mainly the montane zone.

Breeding: In the early spring ♂♂ stake out their breeding territories by singing vigorously, especially in the morning and evening. They staunchly defend them against intruders. Many nests are placed among or under ground-vegetation, and are very well hidden from above. Niches in banks, walls and tree-trunks are also used, while on and within buildings a wide variety of ledges or crevices may be chosen. The materials are moss, dead leaves and grasses with a lining of rootlets, hair and sometimes feathers. The ♀ alone incubates the four to seven eggs, which are white, speckled (sometimes densely) with orangy-red. Incubation and fledging each take about two weeks. Double-brooded as a rule.

Food: The Robin feeds mainly on the ground, on small insects and their larvae, spiders, worms and small snails; it takes berries like those of elder and snowberry in autumn, while in winter it readily comes for kitchen scraps, also taking small seeds or a mixture of fat and bran.

Bluethroat · *Luscinia svecica* (L.) ▷
Red-marked form left, white-marked form right

Family: Thrushes etc. (Muscicapidae) *Subfamily:* Thrushes (Turdinae)
Description: The sexes are alike in plumage except for the throat and

139

breast. The upperparts are olive-brown, with a cream-coloured stripe running above the eye; the sides of the front part of the tail are reddish, the rest of the tail being grey-brown. The belly is greyish-white. The throat and breast of the ♂ are a bright blue. This is demarcated from the belly by a black and a chestnut band. The Scandinavian race has a rusty-red spot in the middle of this blue area, while in the central and south European race the spot is white (or occasionally lacking). The ♀ has a whitish throat bordered with bluish-grey or greyish-brown. Juveniles have light and dark brown spotting, but their tails are coloured like the adults'. L: $5^1/_2''$, Wt: $^2/_3$ oz.

The song usually starts with a high, increasingly fast "dip-dip-dip", followed by mimicry of a variety of other bird voices (e. g. Swallow, Goldfinch, Chiffchaff and Skylark). The chirping of crickets is also imitated; this may in fact be part of the bird's own repertoire of notes. It usually delivers its song from an exposed perch, but also in song-flight, when it spreads out its red-brown tail. "Teck" and "wheet" are the usual call notes.

Distribution: Central Spain, western France, large parts of east and central Europe, Scandinavia, north Persia, the Himalayan region, great stretches of Asia from 40° N to the Bering Sea and across to Alaska. The Bluethroat is a summer visitor and winters in north Africa and southern Asia. A few occur in Britain while on migration.
Habitat: Marshy ground with bushes, swampy margins of lakes and rivers, alder carr, dense riparian scrub.

Breeding: The nest is concealed on the ground, usually sheltered by a grass tussock. It is formed of dead grasses and leaves, rootlets and moss and has a lining of hair, wool or feathers. The clutch contains five to six greyish-green eggs with brownish speckles. Incubation takes 13—14 days and is done by the ♀ alone. The young leave the nest after about two weeks. Normally single-brooded.
Food: Smaller insects and their larvae, spiders and small snails, occasionally also berries in autumn.

Allied species:
The Siberian Rubythroat *(Luscinia calliope)* is found in the taiga-

woods of Russia and in north-east Asia. It generally resembles a Blue-throat but has a ruby-red throat. Its tail is uniformly olive-brown.

Nightingale · *Luscinia megarhynchos* Brehm. Above ▷

Family: Thrushes etc. (Muscicapidae) *Subfamily:* Thrushes (Turdinae)
Description: Both sexes are uniformly brown above with the tail chestnut-brown. The underparts are brownish-white and unmarked, except for a faint scaly effect. Juveniles have a spotted appearance (like young Redstarts) but already have the characteristic chestnut tail. L: 6³/₄″, Wt: *c.* 1¹/₄ oz.

The very distinctive song consists of metallic clucking or throbbing phrases alternating with rich, drawn-out liquid notes: "deoo-deoo-deoo ..." rising in the so-called crescendo. One frequently hears the soft "wheed" call, and a jarring "karr" is used when the bird is agitated.

Distribution: Southern England, the southern half of Europe, Asia Minor, Persia, the Caucasus, the Kirghiz Steppes region and north Africa. It is a summer visitor, spending the winter in tropical Africa.
Habitat: Low-lying deciduous woods, also thickets in more open country and, especially in southern Europe, both damp and dry scrubland.

Breeding: The nest is built in shady places, on or a little above the ground, often in undergrowth near dense thickets, at the base of a bush or between tree-roots or shoots. It is formed largely of dead leaves with a lining of grass stems and hairs. The four to six eggs have a greenish-white ground so densely covered with olive-brown speckles that they appear to be a uniform olive. Only the ♀ sits, hatching out the eggs in 13—14 days. Fledging takes about the same time. Single-brooded.
Food: Smaller insects and their larvae, spiders, small worms, little snails sought among the leaf litter; also berries in autumn.

Thrush Nightingale · *Luscinia luscinia* (L.) Below ▷

Family: Thrushes etc. (Muscicapidae) *Subfamily:* Thrushes (Turdinae)

Description: This species looks very like the Nightingale and is the same size. However, its breast has a distinct dark tinge and the tail is not light chestnut-brown but darker. Juveniles can hardly be distinguished from young Nightingales.

The voice is also similar. However, the songs can be told apart by the fact that the Thrush Nightingale's has no "crescendo" and is even louder and fuller-toned.

Distribution: Denmark, Schleswig-Holstein and Sweden and, above all, eastern Europe and central Russia. Its western limit runs roughly from Hamburg to the Danube delta and here its range sometimes overlaps the Nightingale's, although interbreeding does not occur. It is an extremely rare vagrant to Britain. Like the Nightingale it is a summer visitor, wintering in east Africa.
Habitat: Its haunts are similar to the Nightingale's, but it has an even greater predilection for damp places.
Breeding and *Food*: Very much as in the Nightingale.

Allied species:
The Rufous Bush Chat *(Cercotrichas galactotes)* is found in south-west and south-east Europe, its favourite habitat being opuntia hedges. Its song and the white terminal band on its frequently fanned and twitched tail make it conspicuous.

◁ **Savi's Warbler** · *Locustella luscinioides* (Savi)

Family: Thrushes etc. (Muscicapidae) *Subfamily:* Warblers (Sylviinae)
Description: Both sexes are uniformly brown above, with faint darker barring across the tail. The underside is brownish-white. Juveniles resemble the adults. L: 5^1/$_2$".

Like all *Locustella* warblers, Savi's Warbler likes to sing from exposed perches. The song begins with ticking notes and is a steady reeling, sounding like "tek-tek-urrrrrrr".

Distribution: Southern and eastern Spain, the lower Rhône valley, much of the rest of Europe except Scandinavia and the Baltic states;

north to 55°, eastwards as far as the Caspian Sea and Turkestan. A very few breed in south-east England. It is a summer visitor, wintering in tropical Africa.

Habitat: Reed-beds and rushy areas, marshes bordering lakes and rivers.

Breeding: The nest is usually built among flattened reeds of the previous year or in a tangle of sedges. The sturdy structure of reed leaves is lined with grass stems. The three to five eggs have a whitish ground densely speckled with greyish-brown. Incubation, which is by the ♀ alone, takes about 12 days; the fledging period is about 14 days. Apparently double-brooded.

Food: Small insects and their larvae, spiders.

Allied species:
Two other species of the genus *Locustella* breed in Europe.
The Grasshopper Warbler *(L. naevia)* has a streaked back and its reeling song sounds very like a large grasshopper's. It breeds throughout Britain, except northern Scotland, in rough damp meadows and wasteland, commons and young plantations.
The River Warbler *(L. fluviatilis)* occurs only in eastern Europe (and Asia), inhabiting damp woodland with dense undergrowth. Its song has a grinding quality.

Great Reed Warbler · *Acrocephalus arundinaceus* (L.) ▷

Family: Thrushes etc. (Muscicapidae) *Subfamily:* Warblers (Sylviinae)
Description: Both sexes are uniformly brown above, with a cream-coloured eye-stripe. The underparts are brownish-white. Juveniles are like the adults. L: 7^1/$_2$", Wt: 1 oz.

The song is very loud and harsh, something like "karre-karre-keet-karre-keet . . ."; a gruff "krarr" is used when agitated.

Distribution: All Europe, except the British Isles (to which it straggles on rare occasions), while in Scandinavia it occurs only in southern Sweden; north Africa, Asia Minor, the Caspian depression, and as far as 85° E. A summer visitor, it winters in west, east and south-east Africa.

147

Habitat: Reed-beds by lakes and rivers, also smaller patches of reeds if there are willow thickets close by.

Breeding: The nest is suspended between reed stems, 1½—3 ft above the surface of the water, occasionally higher; it is quite a massive structure with a deep cup of reed leaves and dead stems which the bird wets before weaving them in. It has a lining of finer material. The three to six (usually five) eggs have a greenish-white ground irregularly spotted or blotched with olive-green or olive-brown. They hatch after 13—15 days' incubation, and the young leave the nest when about 12 days old and clamber about on the reeds. One or two broods per year.

Food: This is sought in reed-beds, willow and tamarisk clumps and from the water surface: insects and their larvae, such as dragonflies, tipulids, mayflies, butterflies and beetles, also spiders and sometimes tadpoles and tiny frogs.

◁ **Reed Warbler** · *Acrocephalus scirpaceus* (Herm.)

Family: Thrushes etc. (Muscicapidae) *Subfamily:* Warblers (Sylviinae)
Description: ♂ and ♀ are uniformly brown above and have dingy pale cream eye-stripes. Their entire underparts are brownish-white. Juveniles are similar to the parents. L: 5″, Wt: *c.* ½ oz.

The song is less harsh than the Great Reed Warbler's and sounds more "chatty" with an almost metronome-like rhythm. It may be rendered "chirr-chirr-chirr-jeg-jeg-jeg..." but there are many variations. It occasionally includes quite melodious notes. The ♂ sings either from an exposed position or while sidling among the reeds. When agitated a low "churr" is used, reminiscent of the corresponding call of the Great Reed Warbler.

Distribution: Apart from the very north of England, Scotland, Ireland and most of Scandinavia it breeds all over Europe; also north Africa, Palestine, Cyprus, the Caucasus region, the Caspian depression, and south-west Russia. It is a summer visitor, wintering in tropical Africa.

Habitat: Similar to the Great Reed Warbler's, also small ponds with a narrow strip of reeds, occasionally other aquatic vegetation. It very rarely breeds more than 100 yds from water.

Breeding: The nest is like a Great Reed Warbler's, but considerably smaller. It is usually suspended between reeds, around which the cup of the nest is woven, but the stems of other waterside plants are sometimes used or it may be slung between twigs of small trees at some little distance from water. A clutch contains three to five (most often four) eggs, which have a whitish ground with olive-green spots mainly at the blunt end. Incubation is by both partners, but principally the ♀, and takes 11—12 days. The young leave the nest after 11—12 days, or even sooner, although they are scarcely capable of flight. However, they climb about competently among the reeds in typical *Acrocephalus* warbler fashion. Frequently double-brooded in England.
Food: Smaller insects and their larvae, spiders; elderberries at times in autumn.

Remarks: The Reed Warbler is one of the favourite victims of the Cuckoo. The young Cuckoo grows so fast that it soon protrudes well over the edges of the nest.

Marsh Warbler · *Acrocephalus palustris* (Bechst.)
(Illustration follows p. 155, above)

Family: Thrushes etc. (Muscicapidae) *Subfamily:* Warblers (Sylviinae)
Description: In colour and form both ♂ and ♀ are very like the Reed Warbler, but as a rule are more olive-brown with more yellowish underparts. Juveniles look very like adults. L: 5″, Wt: *c.* ²/₅ oz.

The song is quite different from the Reed Warbler's. In the typical Marsh Warbler song melodious notes and imitations of other bird voices are often masterfully intermingled. Thus one often hears Marsh Warblers which can deceive one by mimicking the songs of Goldfinch, Swallow, Skylark or Great Tit. The actual song—which it usually gives from exposed perches, often in trees—recalls the Bluethroat's, but it lacks that bird's typical "dip-dip . . ." sequences and is usually a few tones higher. The other calls are not unlike the Reed Warbler's.
Distribution: Southern England (where it is very local), north-west and

Reed Warbler · *feeding young Cuckoo* ▷

eastern France, central and eastern Europe northwards to southern Sweden; eastwards between 40° and 60° N as far as 60° E. It is a summer visitor and winters in east and south-east Africa.

Habitat: Rank vegetation with stinging nettles and tall shrubs near water and on swampy ground, also (on the Continent) in open damp woods and in arable fields which may be far from water, and even large gardens with shrubbery.

Breeding: The nest is suspended between plant stems, usually by "basket-handles"; it is shallower than a Reed Warbler's. The general breeding biology is much like the Reed Warbler's, although the spots on the eggs tend to be larger, and it is single-brooded, beginning its breeding very late.

Food: Much as for the Reed Warbler.

Remarks: It is sometimes parasitised by Cuckoos.

Sedge Warbler · *Acrocephalus schoenobaenus* (L.)
(Illustration precedes p. 158)

Family: Thrushes etc. (Muscicapidae) *Subfamily:* Warblers (Sylviinae)
Description: The upperparts of both sexes are olive-brown with dark streaking. The crown is strongly streaked blackish. There is a broad cream-coloured stripe above the eye. The underparts are brownish-white. Young birds resemble the adults. L: 5″, Wt: *c.* ¹/₂ oz.

The song in some ways resembles a Reed Warbler's but is more varied and at times has a more scratchy quality. The bird sings while perched, while moving among vegetation and during short fluttering song-flights. The alarm call heard from agitated birds is "tuc", often rapidly repeated until it sounds like "errr".

Distribution: Most of Europe, including the whole of the British Isles but excluding the Iberian peninsula, southern France, northern Italy and western Scandinavia; Asia above 40° N to about 90° E; a few are found in north Africa. In some areas, especially southern Europe, the distribution has been little studied. It is a summer visitor, wintering in east and south-east Africa.

Habitat: Marshy areas with sedge and rushes, banks of pools and sluggish rivers with willow scrub and reeds, hedges and thorn scrub usually near water but sometimes some distance from it.

Breeding: The nest is generally sited within 2 ft of the ground, often resting on a base of dead grass or other plants. However, like the nests of related species, its sides are attached to plant stems. Nests at greater heights among the twigs of bushes or in thorns are also quite common. It is a slightly untidy structure of moss, grass and plant stems, with a lining of finer grasses, feathers or down. The three to six eggs (very often five) have a whitish ground heavily freckled with yellowish- and greyish-brown, so that they seem an almost uniform fawn colour. Incubation is as a rule only by the ♀, and lasts 12—13 days. Fledging takes just under two weeks. Commonly double-brooded, at least in southern England.

Food: Similar to that of Reed and Marsh Warblers.

Allied species:
Other *Acrocephalus* warblers:
The Aquatic Warbler *(A. paludicola)*, with two dark stripes and a pale stripe between them along the crown, is to be found chiefly in north Germany and eastern Europe.
The Moustached Warbler *(A. melanopogon)*, with a blackish crown, occurs locally in southern and eastern Europe.
Blyth's Reed Warbler *(A. dumetorum)* breeds in north-east Europe.
The Paddyfield Warbler *(A. agricola)* inhabits the Black Sea region.
The tiny Fan-tailed Warbler *(Cisticola juncidis)*, which has brownish upperparts with strong dark streaking, is a characteristic bird of marshy areas in south Europe. It performs undulating flights in wide circles over its territory, accompanying them with unvarying "zip-zip-zip . . ." calls.
The almost uniformly red-brown Cetti's Warbler *(Cettia cetti)* lives on bushy river-banks in southern Europe and western France. Its presence is often revealed by its short but very loud song, which sounds something like "chee-chee-chuyoo".

Marsh Warbler · *Acrocephalus palustris* (p. 151) Above ▷

Icterine Warbler · *Hippolais icterina* (Vieill.) Below ▷
Family: Thrushes etc. (Muscicapidae) *Subfamily:* Warblers (Sylviinae)

Description: Both sexes are light olive-brown above and have a yellowish eye-stripe. The underside is lemon-yellow. Juveniles resemble the parents but have paler underparts. L: 5″, Wt: *c.* ½ oz.

The song is *Acrocephalus* warbler-like, with melodious and discordant sequences. When agitated, the Icterine Warbler utters a "deederoid" call and a chatter.

Distribution: Europe, except the west, the south, and northern Scandinavia; as far east as 85° E; pockets occur south of the Caspian Sea. In Britain it is only a rare visitor at migration times. The bird is a summer visitor, wintering in tropical Africa south of the equator.
Habitat: Open, deciduous or mixed woodland, parks and gardens, occasionally also avenues in larger towns.

Breeding: The nest recalls the *Acrocephalus* type, but is more solidly built and is decorated externally with bits of bark (often birch bark) or scraps of paper. It is usually placed several feet from the ground in the fork of a branch. The material, grasses and small leaves, is woven into a compact felt with wool and cobwebs. The three to five eggs are pink with a few jet-black speckles and spots. Incubation takes 12—14 days, the partners apparently taking turns on the nest. The young fledge after about two weeks. For the most part one brood is reared in a season, although occasional second broods have been recorded in June and July.
Food: Chiefly found in the foliage of bushes and trees: small insects, their larvae, spiders; also berries in autumn.

Allied species:
The Melodious Warbler (*Hippolais polyglotta*) is very like the Icterine Warbler; it too is a rare visitor to Britain, breeding in France, Iberia, Italy and north Dalmatia, also north Africa—especially in dense bush-scrub. Its song recalls the Marsh Warbler's.
The Olivaceous Warbler (*H. pallida*), which is pale earth-brown with creamy-white underparts, occurs in south-eastern Europe and also southern Spain and north Africa.

◁ **Sedge Warbler** · *Acrocephalus schoenobaenus* (p. 154)

The grey-brown Olive-tree Warbler *(H. olivetorum)* is found in Greece, Turkey and Palestine.

The Booted Warbler *(H. caligata)* summers in north-east Europe.

Blackcap · *Sylvia atricapilla* (L.), ♀ ▷

Family: Thrushes etc. (Muscicapidae) *Subfamily:* Warblers (Sylviinae)
Description: The ♂ is greyish-brown above, with a jet-black crown, while the underparts and cheeks are ash-grey. The ♀ is rather more brownish above and has a red-brown crown and pale grey-brown underparts. The young resemble the ♀. L: 5¹/₂″, Wt: ⁷/₁₀ oz.

The typical song is a beautiful warbling, shorter and more stereotyped than the Garden Warbler's, sometimes interspersed with imitations of other birds. The Blackcap's alarm call is a hard "tac" repeated a number of times.

Distribution: The British Isles except north Scotland, all Europe save north and east Scandinavia and the Baltic states, north Africa, southwest Asia and western Russia. The Blackcap is a partial migrant, wintering in the Mediterranean region and north Africa. A very few birds winter in Britain.

Habitat: Open and not excessively dry deciduous and mixed woods with plenty of undergrowth, gullies with scrub-woodland, shrubberies in parks and gardens, overgrown field hedges, also, on parts of the Continent, in bush scrub above the tree limit.

Breeding: The nest is usually built between 1 and 4 ft up among any kind of tangled vegetation or bush twigs; it is a neat but flimsy structure of grass stems and rootlets, often with a lining of hair (plate preceding p. 238, upper). Both sexes incubate the three to six eggs, although the ♀ takes the greater share. The incubation period is about 11 days. The young are not quite ready to fly when they leave the nest at about 11 days (or even earlier if disturbed). Often double-brooded in southern Britain.

Food: Small insects of all sorts and their larvae, spiders; berries in autumn. Over-ripe pears and apples are also pecked into.

◁ **Barred Warbler** · *Sylvia nisoria* (Bechst.)

Family: Thrushes etc. (Muscicapidae) *Subfamily:* Warblers (Sylviinae)
Description: The sexes look very similar. The upperparts are olive-grey or grey-brown, the underparts whitish with dark scaly barring. The eye is bright sulphur-yellow. Juveniles resemble the ♀, except that their underparts are cream-coloured without barring and their eyes are dark. L: 6″, Wt: *c.* 1 oz.

The song is musical and recalls the Garden Warbler's, but may include chattering elements. Alarm is expressed by a harsh churring and a Blackcap-like "tzac".

Distribution: Mainly eastern Europe, the western limits being the upper Rhine valley, the plain of the Po and Denmark; it occurs in Asia to 95° E and as far as 60° N. The Barred Warbler is a summer visitor and winters in east and south-east Africa.
Habitat: Clearings with good undergrowth in deciduous woods, woodland edge with scrub, wild thorny hedgerows, parks. Very dry country is avoided.

Breeding: The nest, an ample sturdy structure of grasses and rootlets, is lined with fine rootlets and hairs. The bird prefers to build it in thorn hedges, but also in various bushes, mostly no more than 3 ft above the ground, though exceptionally at a height of 8 ft. Building is done by both sexes. The four to six eggs have sparse brownish spots on a greenish-grey ground, usually appearing pale grey-green or yellowish-grey. Incubation is by both partners, but mainly the ♀, and takes about 12 days. The young leave the nest when barely two weeks old. Single-brooded.
Food: Insects and their larvae, berries and soft fruit.

Whitethroat · *Sylvia communis* (Lath.)(Illustration follows p. 163, above)

Family: Thrushes etc. (Muscicapidae) *Subfamily:* Warblers (Sylviinae)
Description: In the ♂ the head and nape are grey, the remaining upperparts more or less reddish-brown. The outer tail feathers are white, as is the throat, while the rest of the underside has a pink tinge. The ♀

is a reddish grey-brown above and has cream-coloured underparts, apart from the white throat. Juveniles look like the ♀. L: 5¹/₂", Wt: c. ¹/₂ oz.

The song consists of a hurried, rather scratchy-sounding chatter, and is often given in a fluttering song-flight. When agitated a scolding "churrr" is used, also a nasal "wheeed".

Distribution: Europe, except for northern Scandinavia; north Africa, south-west Asia, and eastwards to longitude 105°. It is a summer visitor, wintering in tropical Africa.
Habitat: Open country with thorny hedges or scrub and rank vegetation (railway embankments are favoured), sunny margins and clearings of woods with bushy undergrowth, occasionally parks and large gardens.

Breeding: The nest is usually placed low above the ground, generally in a thorny tangle, nettles or long grass (see lower plate following p. 239). The three to six eggs are incubated by ♂ and ♀, for about 12 days. The young leave the nest when about 12 days old, unless disturbed earlier. Often double-brooded in Britain.
Food: Much as for the Blackcap.

Whitethroat · *Sylvia communis* ♀ Above ▷

Lesser Whitethroat · *Sylvia curruca* (L.) Below ▷

Family: Thrushes etc. (Muscicapidae) *Subfamily:* Warblers (Sylviinae)
Description: The bird is quite like the Whitethroat, but is greyish-brown above (particularly the ear-coverts), and the head is darker grey. The throat is white like the Whitethroat's and the whitish underparts have a faint pink tinge. The ♀ is paler, showing less contrast in its colouring. Juveniles are like the ♀. L: 5¹/₄", Wt: c. ²/₅ oz.

The song is a quiet warbling with louder phrases sounding like "zizizizizi", also a far-carrying monotonous rattle. Birds indicate alarm by a snapping "tic . . . tic".

Distribution: It breeds over most of England (rarely reaching the Scottish border), also in eastern Wales, but not in Ireland; it extends

over mainland Europe except for the south-west and north Scandinavia, and into Asia to about 120° E. It is a summer visitor, which winters chiefly in east Africa.

Habitat: Open country with clumps of bushes, tall thorny hedges, open scrubby low-lying woodland, sometimes parks and gardens, also dwarf pine scrub in mountain regions.

Breeding: The nest, a small frail structure of fine grasses and rootlets, is usually sited less than 4 ft from the ground, but sometimes at twice this height, among twigs (often brambles). The four to six eggs have a white ground with dark brown spots tending to form a zone near the blunt end. They are incubated by ♂ and ♀, for 11—13 days. Fledging takes 11—12 days. Often double-brooded in England.
Food: Like that of the Whitethroat and Blackcap.

◁ **Garden Warbler** · *Sylvia borin* (Bodd.)

Family: Thrushes etc. (Muscicapidae) *Subfamily:* Warblers (Sylviinae)
Description: ♂ and ♀ are olive-brown above, pale yellowish-brown below, and juveniles look similar. L: 5¹/₂″, Wt: ⁷/₁₀ oz.
    The Garden Warbler's song is a musical, long-sustained and quite loud and variable warbling. The bird shows agitation by "jack-jack" notes, which may develop into a chatter.

Distribution: All Europe, except for the extreme north and south, and as far as 120° E in Asia. It does not breed in northern Scotland, and is uncommon in Ireland. It is a summer visitor, wintering in tropical Africa.
Habitat: Deciduous and mixed woodland with plentiful undergrowth, extensive scrub near water, and locally parks and shrubbery in large gardens.

Breeding: A subdued kind of song, clearly differing from the normal one, is used by the ♂ to advertise the potential nest sites it has selected, where it builds rudimentary "cock's nests". The nest proper is of grass stems, fine twigs and rootlets, usually ¹/₂—3 ft above the ground (sometimes more), in rank, often thorny undergrowth or bushes. The three to six (mostly four or five) eggs have olive-brown flecking on a greenish-white ground; they are incubated by both ♂ and ♀, for 12—13

days. The fledging period 11—12 days. Single-brooded as a rule.
Food: Like that of other *Sylvia* warblers.

Allied species:
Other *Sylvia* warblers, mainly in the Mediterranean region:
The ♂ Orphean Warbler *(S. hortensis)* has a blackish-grey head and white iris. The ♀ has a browner head.
The Sardinian Warbler *(S. melanocephala)* is ash-grey above with a black head and red eye-ring.
The Subalpine Warbler *(S. cantillans)* has a white moustachial stripe.
The Dartford Warbler *(S. undata)* is brownish-red below, grey above; it resides in very small numbers on heathland in southern England, as well as further south.
The Spectacled Warbler *(S. conspicillata)* like a small Whitethroat.
Marmora's Warbler *(S. sarda)* is completely slate-grey, inhabiting western Mediterranean islands.
Rüppell's Warbler *(S. Rüpelli)* breeds in the Aegean region; it is grey above and whitish below, the ♂ having a black head and throat with white moustachial stripe.

Bonelli's Warbler · *Phylloscopus bonelli* (Vieill.) Above ▷

Family: Thrushes etc. (Muscicapidae) *Subfamily:* Warblers (Sylviinae)
Description: ♂ and ♀ are olive-brown above, the rump is pale greenish-yellow and the underparts are whitish, with no tinge of yellow. Juveniles are like the adults. L: 4$^{1}/_{3}$", Wt: $^{1}/_{4}$ oz.
The song is a trill on the same note, like "didididididit". A dissyllabic "hoo-eet" is frequently heard.

Distribution: South-west and southern Europe, south central Europe (roughly south of latitude 50°), north Africa and Asia Minor. Bonelli's Warbler has very seldom been noted in Britain. It is a summer visitor, wintering chiefly in west Africa south of the Sahara.
Habitat: Open pine and larch woods, mixed woods with clearings, especially on south-facing slopes.

Breeding: The nest is placed on the ground, often under a grass tussock. It is a domed structure of grasses and rootlets, with leaves and

Chiffchaff · *Phylloscopus collybita* (p. 170) Below ▷

straws etc. used to make the outside blend in with the surroundings. The clutch contains four to six eggs, whitish with fine brownish spots. Incubation is by the ♀ alone, and takes 13 days. The young fledge when 10—12 days old. Mostly single-brooded.

Food: Small insects, larvae, spiders.

Chiffchaff · *Phylloscopus collybita* (Vieill.)
(Illustration follows p. 167, below)
Family: Thrushes etc. (Muscicapidae) *Subfamily:* Warblers (Sylviinae)
Description: ♂ and ♀ are both olive-brown above, brownish-white with a slight yellowish tinge beneath. The legs are usually dark. Juveniles are like the adults. L: 4¹/₄″, Wt: ¹/₃ oz.

The song consists of a never-tiring "chiff-chaff-chiff-chiff-chaff . . .", interrupted now and then by a few notes which sound like "trrt-trrt-trrt". The call is a soft "hweed", becoming a harder "hweet" when the bird is alarmed.

Distribution: Almost all Europe, apart from northern Scotland, parts of Scandinavia, eastern Spain and Greece; north Africa, south-west Asia, Asiatic Russia north of latitude 50°, as far as 150° E. The Chiffchaff is a partial migrant, with winter-quarters in south-west Europe and the Mediterranean area.

Habitat: Deciduous, mixed and coniferous woodland rich in under-growth, sometimes parks and gardens, up to the tree limit on mountains on the Continent.

Breeding: The nest is usually placed a little above the ground, only rarely touching it or at heights of more than 3 ft, among rank under-growth or brambles (sometimes dense). It is much like that of the Bonelli's Warbler, except that it is well lined with feathers. The four to seven eggs are white with very dark reddish spots. The incubation period is 13—15 days, only the ♀ sitting and feeding the young, which leave the nest after 12—15 days. Frequently double-brooded.

Food: Like that of Bonelli's Warbler; the bird feeds while fluttering among the foliage, and frequently hovers.

◁ **Willow Warbler** · *Phylloscopus trochilus* (L.)

Family: Thrushes etc. (Muscicapidae) *Subfamily:* Warblers (Sylviinae)
Description: The Willow Warbler is very like the Chiffchaff. Its legs

are usually yellowish-brown. The wing formula is the surest way to distinguish between the species: in the Chiffchaff the 2nd primary (counting from the outermost inwards) is noticeably shorter than the 5th, and the 6th has a notch on its inner web like the 5th, whereas in the Willow Warbler the 2nd and 5th are equally long and the 6th is not notched. L: $4^1/_3''$, Wt: $^1/_3$ oz.

The song is a musical, descending sequence which may be rendered something like "ti-ti-ti-ti-ti-tit-tooee-too". It could be compared to a very melodious Chaffinch song. The call is like the Chiffchaff's, but more distinctly dissyllabic—"hooeet".

Distribution: Chiefly the middle and northern latitudes of Eurasia, including the British Isles, all but the south of France, and the southern edge of the Alps. The Willow Warbler occurs very locally in the Pyrenees, and not at all around the Mediterranean. It is a summer visitor, wintering in tropical and southern Africa.
Habitat: Open deciduous and mixed woodland and young plantations, often with bracken; it prefers lighter undergrowth than the Chiffchaff. Also commons, rough farmland hedges and large gardens. Rarely above 3,000 ft up mountains on the Continent.

Breeding: The Willow Warbler's nest resembles the Chiffchaff's but is nearly always well hidden right on the ground. The four to seven (rarely eight) eggs have light reddish-brown spots on a whitish ground. Incubation is by the ♀ alone, and takes 12—14 days. The fledging period is 13—16 days. Predominantly single-brooded.
Food: Similar to the Chiffchaff's.

Wood Warbler · *Phylloscopus sibilatrix* (Bechst.) ▷

Family: Thrushes etc. (Muscicapidae) *Subfamily:* Warblers (Sylviinae)
Description: ♂ and ♀ have greyish-green upperparts, sulphur-yellow throat and breast and white belly. There is a marked yellow eye-stripe. Juveniles resemble the adults. L: 5″, Wt: *c.* $^1/_3$ oz.

The song consists of two different types of phrase, frequently alternated. The best known is a "sib" repeated at increasing tempo until it becomes a trill, sounding like "sib-sib-sibsibsibsirrrr". Also heard is a soft "piu-piu-piu . . .". The trill is given in flight and when among

171

twigs, the "piu..." only when perched. The call-note is also a soft "piu".

Distribution: Most of Europe, but rare in Ireland and the northern Scottish Highlands, and absent from north Scandinavia, most of the Mediterranean seaboard and the western Black Sea coast. However, it breeds on the eastern side of the Black Sea, in the Crimea and European Russia. It is a summer visitor and winters in tropical Africa.

Habitat: Deciduous and occasionally mixed woods (very rarely pure conifer stands), with little undergrowth. It is a characteristic bird of beech woods, also of birch and oak in some areas.

Breeding: The nest is placed among very light cover, often among leaf litter, on the ground; the lining does not usually include feathers. The five to seven eggs are whitish, fairly heavily spotted with blackish-brown. Only the ♀ sits, incubation taking 13—14 days. The young leave the nest after about 12 days. It is generally regarded as having only one brood, but some pairs certainly go on to raise a second.

Food: Broadly similar to that of other leaf warblers.

Allied species:

The Arctic Warbler *(Phylloscopus borealis)* has its range in northern Scandinavia, north-east Europe and large stretches of northern Asia; it has an eye-stripe extending particularly far back, also a faint pale wing-bar.

The Greenish Warbler *(P. trochiloides)* inhabits north-east Europe and large parts of Asia and has bred in north-east Germany. It too has a whitish wing-bar.

◁ **Goldcrest** · *Regulus regulus* (L.)

Family: Thrushes etc. (Muscicapidae) *Subfamily:* Warblers (Sylviinae)
Description: The upperparts are predominantly olive-green; a yellow stripe runs back along the top of the crown, its centre shading to orange-red in the ♂. The stripe is bordered on each side by a black zone. The sides of the head and the underparts are dull greyish-white to pale grey-brown. The young are similar to adults except that there is no stripe on the crown, which is uniform olive-green. This and the Firecrest are the smallest European species. L: 3$\frac{1}{2}$", Wt: *c.* $\frac{1}{5}$ oz.

174

The usual notes are a high "sisisee", while the weak, very high-pitched song sounds like "sisisee-sisisee-sisisiseretet".

Distribution: The Azores, some mountain regions in northern Spain, the Apennines, middle and northern Europe including the British Isles, but excluding northern Scandinavia and large parts of Hungary; parts of south-west Asia, the Himalayan region, central Asia round to China and Japan. In the north it is mainly a partial migrant, while British and central European birds are largely resident.

Habitat: Coniferous woods from sea-level to the tree limit, also mixed woods and sometimes timbered farm- or parkland and gardens with yew trees.

Breeding: The nest is usually placed near the tip of horizontal or drooping branches of conifers (particularly firs). It has a deep cup, chiefly of moss felted together by cobwebs, softly lined with feathers, wool or hair, slung hammock-like between twigs, and often hard to spot. Some are placed in ivy. Occasional nests are within human reach, but many are high up, often 30 ft or more from the ground. Usually only the ♀ broods the eight to eleven eggs, which are white with brownish or reddish speckles. Incubation takes 16 days, rarely less. Fledging takes over two weeks. The Goldcrest is generally double-brooded.

Food: Small insects and spiders are gathered while the bird rapidly hops and flutters, often hovering briefly among the twigs.

Allied species:
The Firecrest *(Regulus ignicapillus)*, which has a black stripe through the eye with a white stripe immediately above, is less restricted to conifer woods. Its song is a whispering "sisisisisiss", getting gradually louder. It is an uncommon visitor to Britain but a very few birds have recently bred in the south; it occurs over most of Europe, except for Scandinavia.

Spotted Flycatcher · *Muscicapa striata* (Pall.) ▷

Family: Thrushes etc. (Muscicapidae) *Subfamily:* Flycatchers (Muscicapinae)
Description: ♂ and ♀ are grey-brown with dark streaks on the crown.

The underside is greyish-white with grey-brown streaks on the breast and throat. Juveniles have light and dark spotting on the upperparts, and look scaly on the throat and breast as the feathers here have blackish edges. L: 5¹/₂″, Wt: *c.* ²/₃ oz.

This bird sits on exposed perches from which it makes short sallies to catch flying insects. The usual calls are a sharp "ist" or "pst" and a hard "tek-tek". The song consists largely of a rhythmical repetition of the former call.

Distribution: Europe apart from northern Scandinavia and north-east Europe; north Africa, western Asia about as far as 110° E. A summer visitor, it winters in tropical and southern Africa.
Habitat: Woods with clearings, parks, gardens, well-timbered farm-land and open country; often near houses.

Breeding: The nest is of grass, rootlets and moss, lined with hair and other soft material, at heights from 4 ft upwards on ledges or in niches provided by walls, rock banks or old trees, also often on trellises or twiggy outgrowths on tree-trunks. The three to six eggs have a greenish-white ground with orange-red spots (see plate p. 241, upper). Incubation is by the ♀ alone, the average period being 13 days. The young fly after about two weeks. Spotted Flycatchers tend to have two broods in the south of their range, and one brood further north.
Food: Principally flying insects, also berries in summer and autumn.

◁ **Pied Flycatcher** · *Ficedula hypoleuca* (Pall.)

Family: Thrushes etc. (Muscicapidae) *Subfamily:* Flycatchers (Muscica-pinae)
Description: In the ♂ the upperparts are black, or may be a dark grey-brown, with white patches on the wing and a white forehead, the underparts being white. The ♀ has markings like those of the ♂, but is grey-brown instead of black above. In winter plumage, i. e. after moulting in summer, the ♂ resembles the ♀. Juveniles have lighter and darker brown spotting above shaped like tear-drops, and dark spots below. L: 5″, Wt: *c.* ¹/₂ oz.

The song goes something like "chitra-chitra-chi-chititit". When agitated, an explosive "tzek" is used, also a "whit" reminiscent of the Swallow's call.

Distribution: The Iberian peninsula; western and northern England, Wales and Scotland as far as the southern Highlands; the Alps, central and north Europe (but not mid- or western France, Belgium or much of the Mediterranean region); north Africa; Russia above 50° N. It is a summer visitor, wintering in tropical Africa.

Habitat: Open deciduous or mixed woodland (especially oak), also orchards and, on the Continent, parkland. It has been induced to nest in open coniferous woods, though not in Britain, by the provision of nestboxes.

Breeding: Being a hole-nester, it uses mainly natural tree holes, old woodpecker holes and nestboxes. On arriving in spring, the ♂ seeks likely sites, which it "advertises" to the ♀ by singing and flying towards them. The nest is usually quite a shallow structure of straws and bark fibres, lined with finer material. The three to eight (generally six) light blue eggs are incubated only by the ♀, hatching in 13—15 days. The young fly after 14—16 days. Normally single-brooded.

Food: It catches flying insects like the Spotted Flycatcher, although it also takes food extensively on the ground, especially in bad weather.

Allied species:
Very like the Pied Flycatcher are:
The Collared Flycatcher *(Ficedula albicollis)*, which breeds mainly in east Europe, extending locally into Germany; the ♂ is black above with a white collar.
Also a closely related form with a less complete collar *(F. semitorquata)* found in north-east Greece. The ♀♀ and the ♂♂ in winter plumage resemble Pied Flycatchers.
The Red-breasted Flycatcher *(F. parva)* breeds in the eastern Alps, eastern Europe, and in large areas of Asia as far as the Pacific coast. It is the size of a small warbler and has a long white patch on each side of the tail. Mature ♂♂ are brownish-red on the breast (rather like a tiny Robin).

Dunnock (Hedge Sparrow) · *Prunella modularis* (p. 182) ▷

Dunnock · *Prunella modularis* (L.) (Illustration follows p. 179)

Family: Accentors (Prunellidae)
Description: ♂ and ♀ are brown above with blackish streaking, and mainly lead-grey below, especially on the breast and throat. The head is also mainly grey. There are blackish streaks on the flanks. Juveniles are yellowish-rust above with large blackish-brown flecks, and have creamy underparts with dark streaks. L: 6″, Wt: $^7/_{10}$ oz.

It has a quick, musical little song, which at a distance reminds one of a Wren's song, although the trills are lacking. Its thin "seet" call-note is often heard, and there is a tinny "dididi" which is heard especially in autumn.

Distribution: All Europe, except the extreme north and south; western Asia. Although British birds are resident, the species is a partial migrant, some Continental birds wintering in central and western Europe, but many moving to the Mediterranean.
Habitat: All kinds of woodland with clearings and thick undergrowth. It is also fond of young plantations and, especially in Britain, is common in parks, farm hedges and gardens.

Breeding: Most nests are between $^1/_2$ and 5 ft above the ground, common British sites are in bushes, hedges, and among brambles or rank vegetation; young spruces are especially favoured on the Continent. Occasional nests are placed on a ledge of a bank. The material is mainly moss and grass, with a foundation of small twigs and a lining of fine grass, hairs, more moss or, less often, feathers. Only the ♀ sits on the three to five (sometimes six) turquoise-blue eggs. Incubation and fledging each take 12—14 days. Usually double-brooded.
Food: Small insects and their larvae, spiders, small snails, also small seeds which are swallowed whole.

◁ **Meadow Pipit** · *Anthus pratensis*. Above

◁ **White Wagtail** (Continental race of Pied Wagtail) · *Motacilla alba* (p. 186) Below

Allied species:
The larger Alpine Accentor *(Prunella collaris)* inhabits the Alps, various European and Asian high mountain ranges and the Atlas; it has a whitish throat spotted with black, and reddish streaks on the flanks.

Meadow Pipit · *Anthus pratensis* (L.) (Illustration precedes p. 182, above)

Family: Pipits and wagtails (Motacillidae)
Description: ♂ and ♀ have olive-brown to olive-grey upperparts, with blackish streaking. The webs of the outer tail feathers are largely white and the underparts are greyish-white with dark streaks. Juveniles resemble the adults. L: 6", Wt: $7/10$ oz.
The Meadow Pipit makes song-flights, in which it flutters upwards calling "sip-sip ..." at an increasing tempo, and then with an even more rapid "si-si-si-si-si-si-siss" glides back down on open wings to land on a raised tussock. The frequently heard call-notes sound like "seep" or "st".

Distribution: The British Isles, central, north and north-east Europe, the Apennines, the Olympus and several other mountain ranges. A partial migrant, it winters in central and western Europe and the Mediterranean area.
Habitat: Moorland, extending well above the tree limit, and rough damp grassland; common on many off-shore islands. It feeds on lower ground in winter.

Breeding: The nest is of moss, grass and rushes, lined mainly with hair; it is hidden on the ground under a tussock of grass or heather. The four to six eggs have a grey-white ground and are generally densely speckled with dark brown. Incubation takes 13 days and is by the ♀ alone. The young leave the nest after 12—14 days. Single- or double-brooded.
Food: Smaller insects and their larvae, spiders, small molluscs (snails), occasionally weed seeds.

Grey Wagtail · *Motacilla cinerea* (p. 187) ▷

183

Allied species:
Further European species of pipit:
The Tree Pipit *(Anthus trivialis)*, less widespread than the Meadow Pipit in Britain, has a slightly browner tinge above and below, and shorter hind-claws. It is a summer visitor, breeding in open woods with clearings, heaths and downland with trees or bush-scrub, and sometimes railway embankments. A nest is shown on p. 240; eggs laid by different ♀♀ vary greatly in colour.
The Rock Pipit *(A. spinoletta)* is dark and fairly large; it breeds on rocky sea-coasts, whereas another form of the same species, the Water Pipit (a paler bird with a marked eye-stripe) breeds high up the mountains of central and southern Europe.
The Tawny Pipit *(A. campestris)*, sandy and almost unstreaked, inhabits waste ground with sparse vegetation (not in the British Isles or Scandinavia).
The Red-throated Pipit *(A. cervinus)*, with brownish-red, streaked breast, occurs in northern Scandinavia.
The Petchora Pipit *(A. gustavi)* has its home in northern Asia but extends into north-east Europe.
Richard's Pipit *(A. richardi)*, a large pipit, breeds from Siberia to China and occurs in Europe only on passage.

Pied Wagtail (and White Wagtail) · *Motacilla alba* L.
(Illustration precedes p. 182)
Family: Pipits and wagtails (Motacillidae)
Description: In the British race *(M. a. yarelli)* the ♂ is black on the crown, back, tail and wings, which have white bars; it has an extensive black bib. The ♀ is greyer on the head and back and has less black on the breast. The forehead, sides of head and neck, and the belly are white in both sexes. In the Continental race both ♂ and ♀ have ash-grey upperparts with black only on the crown. In winter plumage the throat is white, the bib being reduced to a black crescent, and the British bird's back becomes grey. Juveniles are mainly grey with a smudgy dark grey mark on the throat. In all plumages the outer tail feathers are white. L: 7″, Wt: ⁴/₅ oz.
◁ **Blue-headed** (Continental) race of Yellow Wagtail · *Motacilla flava*
(p. 190) ♂

186

The bird is readily noticed through the constant wagging of its long tail and its piercing "tizzik" call. The song is a twittering composed of variously modulated "tizzik" calls and softer notes.

Distribution: Nearly all of Eurasia (the Pied subspecies only in the British Isles), north Africa. It is a partial migrant, the winter range comprising central and western Europe and especially the Mediterranean region.
Habitat: Open country, especially near water, farmyards and roadside banks in farmland, watercourses with bridges, vineyards; sometimes above the mountain tree limit.

Breeding: Nest sites are in niches and shallow holes in walls, sheds, pollard willows, banks, among ivy, etc. The nest is of grass, rootlets and leaves with a hair and feather lining. The four to seven (mostly five or six) eggs, whitish with dark grey and brownish spots, are incubated by both ♂ and ♀. The incubation period is 12—14 days, and the fledging period 14—15 days. Generally double-brooded.
Food: Smallish insects and their larvae (especially water insects and flies), spiders, small crustaceans, molluscs.

Grey Wagtail · *Motacilla cinerea* Tunst. (Illustration follows p. 183)

Family: Pipits and wagtails (Motacillidae)
Description: The upperparts are ash-grey, with a white eye-stripe. The throat is black with a white moustachial stripe in the ♂, and white in the ♀. The remainder of the underside in both is light yellow, getting darker towards the rear. In winter plumage the ♂ has no black on the throat. The young are brownish-grey above, cream-coloured below, shading into citron-yellow towards the rear. L: 7″, Wt: 7/10 oz.

The calls are shrill and sound like "ziseet". In the song, which is made up of twittering notes, these calls are included with various modulations.

Distribution: Europe, except for the greater part of Scandinavia and the north-east; the Azores, Canary Isles, north Africa, south-west Asia

Waxwing · *Bombycilla garrulus* (p. 191) ▷

and large stretches of Asia eastwards to Japan and the Kamchatka peninsula. The Grey Wagtail is a partial migrant, wintering in central and western Europe and the Mediterranean countries.

Habitat: It is more strongly bound to running water than the Pied Wagtail. Its favourite haunts are fast-flowing rocky streams, especially on high ground, but the bird may occur by slow-flowing rivers with weirs, quarries with a trickle of water, occasionally canals or lakes.

Breeding: Ledges or crevices on stream-banks, bridges or walls are selected for nest sites, often close to a waterfall or weir. The nest is like a Pied Wagtail's. The four to six eggs have a yellowish-white ground densely clouded and speckled reddish-brown. Incubation is by both partners and takes 12—14 days. The young leave the nest when 12—13 days old. Mostly two, sometimes even three broods annually.

Food: As for the Pied Wagtail; water insects and their larvae.

Yellow Wagtail · *Motacilla flava* (Illustration precedes p. 186)

Family: Pipits and Wagtails (Motacillidae)

Description: The upperparts are largely olive-green. The head of ♂♂ of the British race *(M. f. flavissima)* is yellowish, in the central European Blue-headed race *(M. f. flava)* it is bluish-grey with a white eye-stripe, in the south-western race *(M. f. cinereocapilla)* ash-grey with no eye-stripe, in the northern race *(M. f. thunbergi)* it has black ear-coverts, and in the south-east European race *(M. f. feldegg)* it is uniformly black. All races have bright yolk-yellow underparts. The ♀♀ are duller in colouration. In winter plumage the upperparts, including the head of most forms, are a yellowish grey-brown. Juveniles are light grey-brown above, light buff below, with an indistinct grey-brown crescent on the breast. L: 6⅓", Wt: ⅗ oz.

"Pseep" and "see" calls are frequently heard, and are interspersed in the song which is a moderately loud twittering.

◁ **Great Grey Shrike** · *Lanius excubitor* (p. 194) Above

◁ **Woodchat Shrike** · *Lanius senator* (p. 195) Below

Distribution: England, Wales, south Scotland, very rare in Ireland: mainland Europe except the extreme north, Asia, the west coast of Alaska, north Africa and Egypt. It is a summer visitor, spending the winter in tropical Africa, or even further south.

Habitat: Damp meadows, pastures and marshy ground, also (in some areas) arable fields and dry heaths.

Breeding: The nest is well hidden on the ground, for preference under a tussock, weed stem or cabbage-leaf etc. It is formed of leaves, grass and rootlets, lined with fine stems and hairs. The five or six eggs have very dense grey-brown markings on a yellow or greenish-white ground. Only the ♀ incubates, for 12—13 days. The young leave the nest after 12—13 days. Usually single-brooded.

Food: Like that of other wagtails; it often feeds near cattle.

Allied species:
The Asiatic Citrine Wagtail *(Motacilla citreola)* has ash-grey upperparts and a yellow head; it is spreading westwards, and has very occasionally wandered to Britain.

Waxwing · *Bombycilla garrulus* (L.) (Illustration follows p. 187)

Family: Waxwings (Bombycillidae)

Description: The upperparts are mainly of a cinnamon tinge, the rump, upper tail-coverts and the greater part of the tail feathers are ash-grey. The head is adorned by a crest which droops down at the rear. The throat is black, bordered on each side by a white moustachial streak, the underparts are reddish-grey with chestnut under tail-coverts. The end of the tail is black with a yellow terminal band. On the wings there is a white bar, and further out a white patch bordered by red waxy "droplets"; a yellow strip, brighter in the ♂, extends from this white patch to the tip of the wing. The ♀ is much like the ♂. Juveniles are brown above, their throat is whitish with grey-brown streaks, and they have an olive-grey breast and whitish belly. The tail and wing markings are as in the adults. L: 7", Wt: *c.* 2 oz.

Red-backed Shrike · *Lanius collurio* (p. 198) ♂ ▷

The flight is starling-like, fast and slightly rolling. The call, "sirr" in varying loudness and pitch, is often heard.

Distribution: Northern Scandinavia, north-east Europe, Siberia as far as the Kamchatka peninsula, Alaska, north-west Canada. It is a partial migrant, wintering in north-eastern central Europe. However, in some "invasion" years, Waxwings wander much further, reaching Britain in quite large numbers.
Habitat: Extensive coniferous, mixed or deciduous forests in the north, particularly larch woods.

Breeding: Waxwings often breed in loose colonies. The nests are at moderate heights up trees and consist of twigs, grass stems, lichens and moss, usually lined with hair. The four or five eggs have a grey-brown ground with dark spots. Little is known of the breeding biology.
Food: In summer almost entirely insects, above all gnats which are caught in flycatcher-fashion; in autumn and winter berries, apples and pears remaining on trees, casually also non-digestible items like bits of bark, tree seeds and small stones which are later regurgitated in pellets.

Great Grey Shrike · *Lanius excubitor* L. (Illustration precedes p. 190)

Family: Shrikes (Laniidae)
Description: ♂ and ♀ are light grey above and have blackish tails with white outer edges. A broad black stripe runs through the eye. The underparts are white, sometimes with a grey scaly pattern. The wings are black and have one or two white patches. The young are like adults but generally greyer and more distinctly barred. L: 9^1/$_2$", Wt: 2^1/$_4$ oz.

A penetrating "trrooee" call is often heard, while the alarm calls used when agitated are a grating "jaaeek" and a chattering. The song is a subdued babbling with imitations of other birds intermingled.

◁ **Starling** · *Sturnus vulgaris* (p. 199)

Distribution: Europe with the exception of the south-east, Italy, the British Isles, and some parts of Scandinavia; Asia apart from the south-east, the extreme north and Asia Minor; Africa above latitude 10° N; North America. It is a partial migrant, wintering largely in mid- and western Europe (occasionally in Britain), also the Mediterranean area.

Habitat: Open country with isolated trees or tree-clumps, woods with clearings, and similar places.

Breeding: The nest is usually built a good many feet up in trees, exceptionally also in tall scrub. It is a sturdy structure of twigs, grasses, moss, rags and bits of paper, lined with hairs and feathers. Forks in fruit trees are a favourite site. The three to eight (usually five or six) eggs are whitish with grey-brown spots. Incubation takes 14—18 days and the fledging period is 19—20 days. Single-brooded.

Food: The Great Grey Shrike has special perches from which it hunts. It often hovers like a Kestrel above the intended victim. It eats insects of all kinds and small vertebrates such as mice, lizards, frogs and small birds. The prey is jammed into the fork of a tree and then battered with the bill.

Woodchat Shrike · *Lanius senator* L. (Illustration precedes p. 190)

Family: Shrikes (Laniidae)

Description: The crown and nape are chestnut, the rest of the upper-parts being black with a white rump. Prominent characteristics are the two large white shoulder-patches and a white mark on the wing. The underside is whitish with a creamy tinge. The ♀ resembles the ♂ but is duller and generally has a slight grey wave-pattern on the breast. Juveniles are brownish with grey wavy barring above and below. L: 6³/₄″, Wt: 1¹/₃ oz.

The Woodchat Shrike often gives croaking or cawing calls like "geh" and "krehk". Its song is a subdued warbling with imitations of other birds interwoven.

Hawfinch · *Coccothraustes coccothraustes* (p. 202) ♂ Above ▷

Greenfinch · *Carduelis chloris* (p. 203) ♂ Below ▷ *SEEN IN THE GARDEN AT KNOSSINGTON. 10·5·75*

SEEN ON THE LAWN AT KNOSSINGTON 12.5.75 ↑

Distribution: Central Europe up to 55° N, the Mediterranean region, north Africa, Cyprus, Palestine and Syria to south-east Persia. This is a summer visitor, wintering in tropical Africa. Occasional birds wander to Britain in spring or autumn.

Habitat: Open country with scattered trees or tree-clumps, field hedges, orchards, and scrub-woodland in southern Europe.

Breeding: The nest is usually placed at a fair height in a tree, but in the Mediterranean region also often in quite low bushes. It is substantially built, of grass stems, roots etc., with fine grasses, hair and wool, sometimes also feathers, for a lining. The four to seven eggs are greenish-white with grey-brown freckles, often forming a zone nearer the blunt end. Incubation is only by the ♀, which is fed by the ♂. The eggs hatch in 15 days and the young leave the nest after 14—16 days. Single-brooded.

Food: Principally insects (grasshoppers, butterflies, beetles), occasionally small vertebrates.

Red-backed Shrike · *Lanius collurio* L. (Illustration follows p. 191)

Family: Shrikes (Laniidae)

Description: In the ♂ the back is red-brown, and the crown, nape and rump are ash-grey. The tail, which is black, has white at each side of the base. It has whitish underparts, suffused with pink. A broad black stripe runs through its eye. The ♀ is rusty brown above, and brownish-white with grey-brown wavy barring beneath. The broad stripe through her eye is dark brown. Juveniles look like the ♀ but are more strongly barred on head and nape. L: 6³/₄″, Wt: 1 oz.

Its frequently-heard call is a hoarse "geh", changing to "gekeke-kek . . ." when excited. Other bird voices are often imitated in the song.

Distribution: Europe, excluding the extreme north and south, the greater part of Asia. In England it now breeds mainly in the south-east,

◁ **Goldfinch** · *Carduelis carduelis* (p. 206) Above

◁ **Siskin** · *Carduelis spinus* (p. 207) ♂ Below

in far smaller numbers than formerly. A summer visitor, it winters in southern Africa.

Habitat: Open country (e. g. commons) with thorny scrub, woodland margins with hedges, neglected field hedges, bushy roadside verges, even parks and large gardens where it is abundant.

Breeding: Its favourite nest site is among thorny scrub, but it may use other bushes or even occasionally trees. It is a typical shrike nest, although less bulky than the Woodchat Shrike's. Only the ♀ broods the four to seven eggs (see plate p. 241, lower). The incubation period is 14—16 days and the fledging period 14—15 days. Single-brooded.

Food: Similar to the Woodchat Shrike's. Larger items of prey are impaled on thorns and then battered with the bill (hence the name "butcher-bird").

Allied species:
The Lesser Grey Shrike *(Lanius minor)* has a black stripe across the forehead; it inhabits the eastern part of south Europe, south-west Asia and Russia.

The Masked Shrike *(L. nubicus)*, which has a black head, white forehead and wine-red flanks, has its home in eastern Greece, south-west Asia and Cyprus.

Starling · *Sturnus vulgaris* (L.) (Illustration precedes p. 194)

Family: Starlings (Sturnidae)
Description: ♂ and ♀ are black all over with an iridescent sheen. The feathers of the crown, back, flanks and under tail-coverts have pale brown or whitish tips. After the summer moult, the whole plumage is covered with small pale spots. This colouring changes to the glossy breeding plumage by abrasion. Juveniles are grey-brown with paler streaks on the breast and a pale throat. L: $8^3/4''$, Wt: $2^2/3$ oz.

Redpoll · *Carduelis flammea* (p. 210) Above ▷

Citril Finch · *Carduelis citrinella* (p. 211) ♂ Below ▷

The call note is a harsh "schair"; in alarm a sharp "bett-bett" and a hoarse "rah" are given. The song is a throaty babbling incorporating loud whistles and numerous imitations of other animal sounds.

Distribution: Europe, excepting the extreme north-east, Spain, southern Italy and southern Greece; large areas of Asia. It has been introduced and spread widely in North America and Australia. This is a partial migrant, wintering in western Europe and the Mediterranean region.
Habitat: Woods of all kinds, farmland, parks, orchards, built-up areas. Out of the breeding season the birds roost in large flocks in reed-beds, among trees and (in Britain) on buildings in some city-centres.

Breeding: Starlings are hole-nesters, occupying holes in trees, buildings or rocks, and often nesting socially. The nest is an untidy, shallow structure of straws, leaves and feathers. Both ♂ and ♀ incubate the three to eight sky-blue eggs, which hatch after 12½—13 days. The young fly after about 20 days. In the north mainly single-brooded, further south many pairs rear two broods in some seasons.
Food: Insects and their larvae, spiders, worms, berries and fruit.

Allied species:
The Rose-coloured Starling *(Sturnus roseus)* with pink and black plumage breeds in eastern Europe.
The uniformly black, glossy Spotless Starling *(S. unicolour)* inhabits the Mediterranean region.

Hawfinch ·*Coccothraustes coccothraustes* (L.)(Illustration follows p. 195)

Family: Finches (Fringillidae)
Description: The massive bill is the most remarkable feature. ♂ and ♀ are predominantly brown above with a grey band across the nape, the throat is black and the underparts light brown. The tail has a white terminal band. There is a large white patch on the wing and the black

◁ **Twite** · *Carduelis flavirostris* (p. 214) Above

◁ **Linnet** · *Carduelis cannabina* (p. 215) ♂ Below

primaries have curiously broadened tips. The ♀ is considerably duller than the ♂. Juveniles are largely brownish with greyish-brown spots on the breast. L: 7″, Wt: 2 oz.

The call notes are a sharp "zick" and a high-pitched "zeee", which frequently recur in the song, which is a subdued, tinny twittering.

Distribution: Europe except in the north, north Africa, the northern part of the Middle East, Russia, Mongolia, northern China, Japan. In England and Wales it is quite widespread but local, often overlooked because it is very shy. It is a partial migrant, wintering in west-central Europe and the Mediterranean area.
Habitat: Open deciduous and mixed woods (especially oak-hornbeam woods), parks, orchards and well-timbered farmland.

Breeding: The nest, usually at a fair height up a tree—in a fork or out on a limb—is of twigs and rootlets lined with soft plant material and grass. The four to six eggs are bluish-white with grey-brown and blackish spots. Incubation takes 12—14 days and is done largely by the ♀, occasionally relieved by the ♂. The young fly after a similar period. Normally single-brooded.
Food: In the breeding season chiefly insects and their larvae, on which the young are almost exclusively reared; outside the breeding season, it takes plant and tree seeds, cracking cherry and plum stones for their kernels.

Greenfinch · *Carduelis chloris* (L.) (Illustration follows p. 195)

Family: Finches (Fringillidae)
Description: The ♂ is predominantly moss-green, with a yellowish rump. Its primaries and tail are partially yellow. The ♀ is patterned like the ♂ but is browner above and greyer below. The young resemble the ♀, apart from being diffusely streaked on the breast and back. L: 6″, Wt: 1 oz.

The song, given in bat-like song-flight, may be rendered "cheechee-cheechee-kreerrrr-deudeudeudeudeudeudeudeut" It also sings while per-

Serin · *Serinus serinus* (p. 215) ♂ ▷

ched, and then often adds a nasal "deeeng". A trilling "geerrr" may also be heard.

Distribution: Europe, except for the extreme north and north-east, north Africa and south-west Asia round to 60° E. In the north it is a partial migrant, while in mid- and southern Europe it is a resident.
Habitat: Parkland, gardens, field hedges, woodland margins and scrub, clumps of conifers, evergreen shrubberies.

Breeding: A favourite nest site is in a thick hedge (hawthorn, briar, privet, etc.), but shrubs and creepers are often chosen too. The usual height-range is 4—12 ft from the ground, nest material being moss, twigs and grass with wool and hair for lining. The four to six (rarely three or seven) eggs, whitish with reddish-brown and blackish spots, are incubated only by the ♀, who is fed by the ♂ with food regurgitated from the crop. The eggs hatch in 12—15 days and the fledging period is 13—16 days. Two broods a year are frequently reared, in odd cases a third.
Food: Greenfinches are vegetarians, living on seeds, particularly unripe ones, buds, leaf-tips and yellow flowers; sometimes also greenfly and caterpillars in the breeding season.

Goldfinch · *Carduelis carduelis* (L.) (Illustration precedes p. 198)

Family: Finches (Fringillidae)
Description: Both ♂ and ♀ have a light brown back and white rump. The crown is black, the cheeks are white and the "face" from forehead to chin red. There is a conspicuous yellow bar along the black wings. The underparts are whitish with a pale brown wash on the sides of the breast. Juveniles have a similar patterning to the adults, except for the head which is buffish streaked with greyish-brown; their underparts are also streaked. L: 4³/₄″, Wt: ³/₅ oz.

The Goldfinch has a rather high-pitched musical "slee-witz" call-note The song is a lively twittering, interspersed with modified forms of the call. In the presence of danger the "ahee" alarm note is used.

◁ **Bullfinch** · *Pyrrhula pyrrhula* (p. 218) ♂

Distribution: Europe, except the extreme north and north-east; north Africa, south-west Asia, eastwards to India and the central Russian steppes. It is a partial migrant which winters in mid- and southern Europe.

Habitat: Open country with tree-clumps, parkland, tall hedges, orchards, thin mixed woodland with clearings. It is very fond of weed-covered waste land.

Breeding: The majority of nests are well out of reach in trees (often fruit trees) and often near the tips of boughs. The nest is a beautiful, neat structure of grass, fibres, moss and much plant-down (especially from poplar seeds if available), lined with hairs and wool. The three to six eggs are white with dark reddish spots. Incubation, which is by the ♀ alone, takes 12—14 days. The young stay in the nest for about 15 days. Frequently double-brooded.

Food: Weed and tree seeds, particularly when unripe; in the breeding season small insects like greenfly, Diptera and small beetles are taken too.

Siskin · *Carduelis spinus* (L.) (Illustration precedes p. 198)

Family: Finches (Fringillidae)

Description: The upperparts are yellowish-green, with yellow rump and some yellow on the tail. The ♂ has a greyish-black crown and often also a blackish chin. The ♀ has a greyish-green head. The underside is pale yellowish-green with dark streaks along the flanks in the ♂, and dingy greyish-yellow with darker streaks in the ♀. Juveniles are like the ♀ but greyer. L: 4³/₄″, Wt: *c.* ¹/₂ oz.

Frequently heard calls are a loud, plaintive "deeay" and a hard "tetetetet". The song is a lively twittering, mostly ending with "deedldeedldaitch".

Distribution: Chiefly east-central Europe, eastern and northern Europe apart from northern Scandinavia; in the south it is largely confined to high ground such as the Pyrenees, while it breeds sparingly over northern Britain and Ireland; the range also includes central Russia, northern China, Japan. It is a partial migrant, wintering in mid- and

Crossbill · *Loxia curvirostra* (p. 219) ♂ ▷

southern Europe (fair numbers winter in England, where it has begun to breed too).

Habitat: It breeds in coniferous forests, especially in mountain country. Outside the breeding season it occurs in lowland woods, among alder and birch trees by water, and also in parks and gardens.

Breeding: As a rule the nest is sited among dense twigs high up in conifers; it is artistically built of moss, grass and small twigs, often adorned with lichens, and lined with hair, wool, sometimes also feathers. The four to six eggs are very like Goldfinches'. Incubation is all done by the ♀, which is fed by the ♂, and takes 11—14 days. The young leave the nest after 13—15 days. Single- or double-brooded.
Food: Chiefly the seeds of trees (alder, birch, spruce, pine), weed seeds, buds, pollen from willow-catkins, and small insects (caterpillars, aphids).

Redpoll · *Carduelis flammea* (L.) (Illustration follows p. 199)

Family: Finches (Fringillidae)
Description: The upperparts are largely greyish-brown with dark streaks, the forehead being red and the chin black. In the ♂ the throat and breast and also the rump have a pink tinge, which is lacking in the ♀. Juveniles are like the ♀ without the chin-spot and red forehead. L: 5″, Wt: *c.* ¹/₂ oz.

A rattling "chi-chi-chi" call is often heard, especially in flight. The song is somewhat reminiscent of a Greenfinch's, although softer and without the "deeng".

Distribution: The British Isles (where the birds are slightly smaller and darker than Continental and northern forms), the Alps, some east-European mountain ranges, northern Europe, part of Iceland and the coast of Greenland, almost all of Asia above 50° N, northern North America. It is a partial migrant, wintering in central and western Europe.
Habitat: Birch and alder woods in the north, conifer (especially larch) woods in the mountains, subalpine alder and willow scrub. In Britain

◁ **Yellowhammer** · *Emberiza citrinella* (p. 222) ♂

Redpolls breed in all these habitat types and also in young plantations.

Breeding: The nest is compactly built of small twigs, grass stems, rootlets and moss with a lining of hair, wool and feathers. It is often placed quite high up in a birch, conifer or other tree, but may be only 4 ft up in a bush or sapling; many nests are artfully camouflaged to blend with the fork in which they are sited. The three to six (usually four or five) eggs, light greenish-blue with brownish spots, are incubated only by the ♀, which is fed by the ♂. The incubation period is about 11 days, and the fledging period 12—15 days. Double-brooded as a rule.

Food: The seeds of birch, alder, larch, and other trees, weed seeds; small insects (aphids, larch tortrix moth caterpillars) in the breeding season.

Citril Finch · *Carduelis citrinella* (Pall.) (Illustration follows p. 199)

Family: Finches (Fringillidae)

Description: The upperparts are a grey-tinged yellowish-green with indistinct dark streaking, the crown and nape are grey, the rump greenish-yellow. The underparts are yellowish-green, with obscure darker streaks in the ♀. Juveniles resemble the ♀ but are more heavily streaked above and below. L: 4³/₄″, Wt: *c.* ¹/₂ oz.

The call-note is a nasal "dit-did". The song recalls that of the Goldfinch, but also contains Serin-like phrases.

Distribution: The higher mountain ranges of central and south-west Europe. It is a partial migrant and winters in southern Europe.

Habitat: Open coniferous (especially fir) woods with sunny clearings, meadows with largish clumps of firs.

Breeding: The ♂ makes frequent bat-like song-flights. The nest is usually a good many feet above the ground in a fir tree, built of grass, twiglets, lichens, moss and rootlets with hairs, wool and feathers for lining. The four or five eggs are bluish-green with red-brown spots,

Cirl Bunting · *Emberiza cirlus* (p. 223) ♂ ▷

and are incubated entirely by the ♀, hatching in about 14 days. The young leave the nest when 17—18 days old. Single- or double-brooded. *Food:* Weed seeds (especially unripe ones), fir seeds, small amounts of algae and lichens, small insects (caterpillars, aphids).

Twite · *Carduelis flavirostris* (L.) (Illustration precedes p. 202)

Family: Finches (Fringillidae)
Description: The bird is buffish-brown above with dark brown streaks, the rump being tinged pink in the ♂. The underside is buffish-white with dark streaking. Both sexes have yellow bills in winter. Juveniles resemble the ♀, although they are more strongly streaked on the breast. L: 5″, Wt: *c.* ²/₃ oz.

The usual calls are "dweedweedwee" and a nasal "chooee". The song, a not very loud twittering, is strung together from these calls with some whistling notes incorporated.

Distribution: It breeds locally in Britain, chiefly in the Pennines, the Scottish Highlands and islands, and parts of Ireland. The rest of its range comprises north-west Scandinavia, mountains between the Black and Caspian Seas, central Asia. A partial migrant, it winters largely in north- and west-central Europe, sometimes wandering to the Mediterranean.
Habitat: Moorland (usually with heather) in Britain; abroad, also stony country with low vegetation. Outside the breeding season it is usually found on waste or fallow ground, also coastal saltings.

Breeding: Nests are often built in loose colonies, in heather or low bushes, under tussocks on banks, or in rock-crevices. The nest and eggs and general breeding biology are much as in the Linnet, although Twites begin breeding later. Double-brooded.
Food: Principally plant and weed seeds and sometimes caterpillars.

◁ **Reed Bunting** · *Emberiza schoeniclus* (p. 226) ♂ Above

◁ **Corn Bunting** · *Emberiza calandra* (p. 227) Below

Linnet · *Carduelis cannabina* (L.) (Illustration precedes p. 202)

Family: Finches (Fringillidae)
Description: The ♂ is chestnut-brown above with a grey-brown head and a pale grey wing-bar. In summer the forehead and breast of the ♂ become red, due to abrasion of the brownish feather-tips. These parts are brownish-grey with darker streaking in the ♀, which is duller brown above. Both sexes have some white on the tail feathers; they are more nearly alike after moulting in summer. Juveniles are like the ♀. L: 5″, Wt: *c.* ²/₃ oz.

The familiar Linnet often attracts notice by its twittering "gigigigig" calls, which occur in the song as well. The song also includes clear musical and chirping notes.

Distribution: All Europe with the exception of north Scandinavia; north Africa, south-west Asia, round to central Asia. This is a partial migrant, wintering in western, middle and southern Europe.
Habitat: Open country with bushes, especially commons, downland and waste ground with gorse or hawthorn scrub, farmland hedgerows, large gardens; on the Continent also vineyards, alpine meadows and sparsely vegetated stony ground.

Breeding: The bird prefers to build its nest in thorny bushes or thick hedges, at heights up to 6 ft, using small twigs, grasses, rootlets and shreds of bark with a lining of wool, hair and down. The four to six eggs are like small Greenfinch eggs, although they sometimes have a slight blue tinge. Incubation is all done by the ♀, and takes 11—13 days. The fledging period is about 14 days. Generally double-brooded.
Food: Principally weed seeds, which are fed to the young from the crop; occasionally also small insects and spiders.

Serin · *Serinus serinus* (L.) (Illustration follows p. 203)

Family: Finches (Fringillidae)
Description: The ♂ is yellowish grey-green above with grey-brown streaks. The forehead and rump are yellow, as is the breast. The flanks

Rock Bunting · *Emberiza cia* (p. 230) ♂ ▷

and sides of the breast are lightly streaked. The ♀ has less yellow and is more heavily streaked and spotted. Juveniles resemble the ♀. L: *c.* 4²/₃", Wt: *c.* ¹/₂ oz.

The call-note is a tinkling "gerrlitt", the song a succession of trills; it is often given during a bat-like display-flight, but also while perched.

Distribution: Europe, with the exception of the British Isles and all but the very south of Scandinavia; north Africa, Asia Minor. The bird has gradually spread westwards in Europe, and now reaches England (where it recently bred for the first time) with increasing frequency. It is a partial migrant, wintering mainly in southern Europe.
Habitat: Open country with copses, deciduous and mixed woods with plenty of clearings, hedgerow timber, parks and gardens.

Breeding: The nest is usually sited at moderate heights in trees, often also lower down in sites like cypresses in cemeteries or gooseberry bushes in gardens. It is a small cup of grasses, rootlets and plant-down, lined with hair and wool. The three to five eggs have a bluish-white ground with rusty and dark brown spots. Incubation is by the ♀ alone, the period being 12—14 days. The young fly after 14—16 days. Normally double-brooded.
Food: Small seeds, especially when unripe, soft leaf-tips. The Serin appears to be a pure vegetarian. Nestlings are fed with a "mash" of partly digested seeds.

Bullfinch · *Pyrrhula pyrrhula* (L.) (Illustration precedes p. 206)

Family: Finches (Fringillidae)
Description: The ♂ is grey above with a white rump and a glossy black cap. Its breast and cheeks are bright red, and its belly white. The ♀ has a more greyish-brown back and a brownish-grey breast. Juveniles are rather like the ♀ except that their cap is olive-brown instead of black. L: 6", Wt: 1 oz.

◁ **Little Bunting** · *Emberiza pusilla* (p. 231) Above

◁ **Snow Bunting** · *Plectrophenax nivalis* (p. 231) Below

Its piping "phiu" or "bit" calls are often heard. The song, by both sexes, sounds like a plaintive piping "di-dee-deeoo".

Distribution: Central and northern Europe, including the British Isles but excluding northernmost Scandinavia; the Pyrenees, the Italian peninsula, the Balkans, mountain regions between the Black and Caspian Seas; large stretches of Asia above 50° N round to Japan. Northern populations are partially migrant, mid-European birds are mainly sedentary.

Habitat: Woodland and copses with plenty of scrub (conifer woods in north Britain and the Continent), also field hedges and shrubberies in large gardens, orchards in winter.

Breeding: The nest, which is built at no great height in (often thorny) shrubs or hedges, is a shallow structure of twigs lined with rootlets and hairs. The three to six eggs have a pale bluish or whitish ground sparsely marked with black and diffuse reddish-brown spots. Incubation is by the ♀ alone and takes about 13 days. The fledging period is about 16 days. Generally double-brooded.

Food: Seeds of all kinds, also buds (especially flower-buds from fruit-trees, which are taken when seeds are scarce), small insects, particularly caterpillars and spiders.

Allied species:

The Scarlet Grosbeak *(Carpodacus erythrinus)* breeds in north-east Europe and large areas of Asia; the ♂ has a carmine head and breast, the ♀ is greyish-brown with streaked underparts.

The Pine Grosbeak *(Pinicola enucleator)* is almost Starling-sized, and has two white wing-bars. The ♂ is largely pinkish-red, the ♀ greenish-brown. It occurs in northern Scandinavia, north-east Europe, northern Asia as far as the Kamchatka peninsula and in North America.

Crossbill · *Loxia curvirostra* L. (Illustration follows p. 207)

Family: Finches (Fringillidae)
Description: The head and body of the mature ♂ are largely brick-red,

Brambling · *Fringilla montifringilla* (p. 235) ♂ ▷

the wings and tail being dark grey-brown. The ♀ is greyish-green, darker above and paler with indistinct streaking below. Young birds resemble the ♀ but are more heavily streaked. L: 6¹/₃", Wt: c. 1¹/₂ oz.

The much-used call-notes are a ringing "chip-chip", and there is also a nasal "tuk-tuk". The song is made up of these calls with wheezing, whistling and chinking notes too.

Distribution: Central, southern and eastern Europe, chiefly mountain areas (in Britain resident in parts of the Scottish Highlands, also East Anglia), much of Scandinavia, north Africa, Asia Minor, most conifer-forest areas of Asia, as far as Japan. It is a resident but in certain years of food-shortage moves in large numbers into new areas; many birds may then be seen in the British Isles and some stay and breed in various places.

Habitat: Coniferous and mixed forests, especially with fir trees; the Scottish race inhabits pine forests.

Breeding: The Crossbill may breed at any time of the year, but mainly from December to May. It builds its nest in conifers, at a considerable height from the ground; this is a stout structure of twigs, grass stems, lichens and moss; the rather deep cup is lined with fine grasses. The three or four eggs have a greenish-white ground with reddish and blackish spots. They are brooded only by the ♀, which is fed by the ♂. Incubation takes 14—16 days and begins with the laying of the first egg. The birds carry on breeding undeterred by cold or snow. Single- or double-brooded.

Food: Seeds extracted from the cones of fir, pine and larch, also other tree and weed seeds, buds, small insects, and in winter often particles of ash, saltpetre (from masonry) and urine (from middens etc.).

Allied species:
The larger and stouter-billed Parrot Crossbill *(Loxia pytyopsittacus)* breeds in Scandinavia and north-east Europe.
The Two-barred Crossbill *(L. leucoptera)*, with two white wing-bars, inhabits north-east Europe, Siberia and North America.

Yellowhammer · *Emberiza citrinella* L. (Illustration precedes p. 210)

Family: Finches (Fringillidae)

Description: The rump is chestnut, the remaining upperparts, apart from the head, are warm brown with heavy dark streaking. The head of the ♂ is bright yellow (concealed by grey-brown feather-tips in autumn) with brownish marking in the region of the ear. The ♀ has less yellow on the head, and is generally more sombre-hued. Both have yellowish underparts with a brown-tinged breast, more heavily streaked in the ♀. Juveniles resemble the ♀. L: 6½″, Wt: *c.* 1 oz.

The song has a slightly melancholy quality and sounds like „dididi-dididit-zeee" (popularly expressed as "a-little-bit-of-bread-and-no-cheese"). The calls are a sharp "zick" and, when taking flight, "zickerr".

Distribution: Europe, except for the extreme north and south, large regions of Asia above 50° N. It is a partial migrant, wintering in mid- and southern Europe. British birds are resident.

Habitat: Open country with scattered trees or bush scrub (e. g. bushy commons and downs), banks and rough hedgerows in farmland, vineyards. In winter it is often seen in small flocks in fields, and visits stackyards and middens.

Breeding: The nest of grass, plant stalks, moss and rootlets, lined with hair, is generally low down among tangled herbage but may be several feet up in a thorn-bush or hedge, or on the ground: ditch-banks are favourite sites. The three to five eggs are whitish with dark purplish scribbles and spots. Incubation, which is by the ♀ alone, takes 11—13 days. The young leave the nest after 10—14 days. Normally double-brooded.

Food: Seeds, insects, especially grasshoppers and moths, small snails. The nestlings are raised entirely on insects.

Cirl Bunting · *Emberiza cirlus* L. (Illustration follows p. 211)

Family: Finches (Fringillidae)
Description: The upperparts are quite like the Yellowhammer's, but the rump is olive, not chestnut. The head of the ♂ is not completely yellow, but grey-brown with yellow sides to the face and a narrow

Chaffinch · *Fringilla coelebs* (p. 238) ♂ ▷

black stripe through the eye; the chin and throat are black. A greyish-green band divides off the yellow of the upper breast from the yellowish-white of the remaining underparts. The ♀ resembles a ♀ Yellowhammer but is greyer. Juvenile plumage is very like that of the ♀. L: 6⅓″, Wt: 1 oz.

The song is a repetition of one slightly grating note, sounding something like "drilililililililil". There is also a thin "seee" call.

Distribution: Southern Europe (including the south of England), Asia Minor, north Africa, in central Europe only in very warm places. It is predominantly a resident, and does not wander far.
Habitat: Warm, dry open country with scattered bushes and trees, also hedges, vineyards on the Continent.

Breeding: The nest resembles a Yellowhammer's and is usually placed within a few feet of the ground in a hedge, bush or undergrowth. The two to six eggs are very like Yellowhammers'. The ♀ alone incubates. The young hatch out after 11—13 days and stay in the nest for 10—13 days. Usually double-brooded.
Food: Weed seeds; chiefly insects in the breeding season.

Reed Bunting · *Emberiza schoeniclus* L. (Illustration precedes p. 214)

Family: Finches (Fringillidae)
Description: The back is brown with blackish streaks, the rump grey-brown and the underparts greyish-white with dark streaks (more in the ♀ than the ♂). The ♂ has a black head, throat and upper breast, and a white collar which continues forward on each side as a moustachial streak. The ♀ lacks these features; its head is predominantly greyish-brown with a pale eye-stripe and moustachial streak and dark ear-coverts. After the summer moult the ♂ resembles the ♀ since brown feather-tips hide the black of the head. Young birds look like the ♀. L: 6″, Wt: *c.* ⅔ oz.

◁ **Chaffinch** · *Fringilla coelebs* (p. 238) ♀ Above

◁ **Italian Sparrow** · *Passer italiae* (p. 242) ♂ Below

The song sounds "stuttering" and may be rendered "tee-ti-tai-zississ". The commonest call-note is a high-pitched "zeee", recalling a Yellow Wagtail's note.

Distribution: Europe and large regions of Asia. A partial migrant, the Reed Bunting winters in mid- and southern Europe; British birds show little movement.

Habitat: Swampy ground, damp rushy meadows, waste ground by gravel pits, reed-beds; sometimes on farmland away from water.

Breeding: The nest is placed on the ground, well hidden under a tussock of grass or rushes, or less often in vegetation a little off the ground; it is not very substantially built, of grass, reed leaves and similar material, lined with fine grasses and hair. The three to six eggs have a pale buffish ground with dark spots and squiggles. Incubation is by the ♀ alone, the period being 12—14 days. The young stay in the nest for 10—13 days. Generally double-brooded, at least in the southern part of the range.

Food: Predominantly insects in the breeding season (the young are fed entirely on them); also small snails, various crustaceans and spiders, seeds of weeds, reeds and sedges.

Corn Bunting · *Emberiza calandra* L. (Illustration precedes p. 214)

Family: Finches (Fringillidae)
Description: ♂ and ♀ are grey-brown above with dark streaks, and off-white below with rows of dark streaks. Juveniles are similar to the adults but are more streaked. L: 7″, Wt: 1³/₄ oz.

The Corn Bunting sings from an exposed perch; the song, "zick-zick-zickzickzick-zrrrrrrps", is usually likened to the jangling of a bunch of keys. The call, often heard in flight, is a sharp "zick".

Distribution: Europe with the exception of all but the extreme south of Scandinavia and the Baltic States; north Africa, and the Middle East to Persia and Turkestan. It is a partial migrant, wintering in western, central and southern Europe.

House Sparrow · *Passer domesticus* (p. 239) ♀ ▷

Habitat: Corn and arable fields, open downland with occasional trees, bushes or telegraph poles, sometimes waste or swampy ground, in southern Europe also dense bush scrub with clearings and desert scrub.

Breeding: The nest is made from grass stems, roots and small leaves, lined with hairs, sometimes also odd feathers. It is usually sunk into a hollow in the ground, often among growing crops, but may be a few inches above the ground among vegetation. The three to five (rarely six) eggs are whitish with dark spots, scribbles and hairlines. Only the ♀ incubates; the ♂ (who is sometimes polygynous) escorts her to and from the nest to feed. The eggs hatch in 12—14 days and the young leave the nest after 9—12 days. Probably single-brooded as a rule, but second broods may be more frequent in the south.

Food: Weed seeds, grain, insects (including many grasshoppers) and small snails.

Rock Bunting · *Emberiza cia* L. (Illustration follows p. 215)

Family: Finches (Fringillidae)

Description: The ♂ has the head, neck and upper breast ash-grey, with black stripes above and through the eye and a black moustachial streak. The rest of the underside, the lower back and rump are all cinnamon-coloured, while the back is greyish-brown with dark streaks. The ♀ is similarly patterned but browner with finely streaked throat and upper breast. Young birds resemble the ♀. L: 6¹/₃″, Wt: *c.* ⁷/₁₀ oz.

The Rock Bunting's call is a drawn-out "zeep". The song recalls those of both Dunnock and Reed Bunting.

Distribution: Chiefly south and south-east Europe, in mid-Europe extending as far as 50° N in the Rhine valley; North Africa, Asia Minor, central and south-east Asia. Predominantly resident.

Habitat: Rocky, sun-favoured regions with bush scrub, especially hillsides with boulder-scree, and terraced vineyards.

◁ **House Sparrow** · *Passer domesticus* (p. 239) ♂

Breeding: The Yellowhammer-like nest is mostly situated on the ground beneath a small bush, among vegetation, in rock-crevices, or under boulders. The three to five eggs are greyish-white with occasional dark spots and interlacing hairlines. The young hatch after 12—13 days' incubation, which is by the ♀ alone, and leave the nest 10—13 days later. Mainly double-brooded.
Food: Insects during the breeding season; also weed seeds.

Little Bunting · *Emberiza pusilla* Pall. (Illustration precedes p. 218)

Family: Finches (Fringillidae)
Description: The Little Bunting is like a small female Reed Bunting, although the crown and cheeks are reddish-brown. The ♀ is somewhat duller than the ♂; juveniles resemble the ♀. L: *c.* 5".

The song is a quiet, rather stammering yet melodious twitter. There is also a sharp "zick" call-note.

Distribution: North-east Europe, north Scandinavia, northern Asia. It is a partial migrant, wintering occasionally in mid- and south Europe, but mainly in Turkestan, India and China. It is a rare wanderer to Britain.
Habitat: The subarctic birch zone, tundra scrub, locally in northern conifer forests.

Breeding: The nest is placed on the ground under grass tussocks or in similar sites. Few details are known about the breeding biology.
Food: Small insects and their larvae, weed seeds.

Snow Bunting · *Plectrophenax nivalis* (L.) (Illustration precedes p. 218)

Family: Finches (Fringillidae)
Description: The ♂ is to a large extent white, with black wing-tips. In winter its crown and ear-coverts are tinged buff and there are grey-brown streaks down its back. The ♀ is basically similar but is considerably browner. Juveniles are similar in plumage to the ♀, but are more heavily streaked above and below. L: 6½", Wt: *c.* 1 oz.

Tree Sparrow · *Passer montanus* (p. 242) ▷

Call-notes include a dissyllabic "tihee", a subdued "trr" and a Linnet-like "gigigig". The song is a short trilling, somewhat reminiscent of the Skylark's song.

Distribution: Northern Scandinavia, a few in the eastern Scottish Highlands, Iceland, arctic regions of Asia and America, the coast of Greenland. Its most southerly breeding area is the Kamchatka peninsula. It is a partial migrant, generally moving no further than 35° N, and chiefly wintering in coastal areas; it is locally not uncommon in Britain in autumn and winter.

Habitat: Rocky arctic coasts, rocky tundra with sparse vegetation, barren ice-free ground, also near buildings in the far north.

Breeding: The nest, generally in a rock-fissure or tunnel among boulders and sometimes in a hole in a wall, has a thick lining of feathers. The four to seven eggs are yellowish- or bluish-white with large reddish-brown spots. Two broods may be reared in Scotland, but in the far north there is only time for one.

Food: Insects, weed seeds, grain, sprouting seeds, household scraps.

Allied species:

A further 6 buntings breed in Europe:

The Black-headed Bunting *(Emberiza melanocephala)*, with black head and yellow breast, in south-east Europe and south-west Asia.

The Yellow-breasted Bunting *(E. aureola)* in north-east Europe and northern Asia.

The Ortolan Bunting *(E. hortulana)*, which has a grey head and yellowish-white eye-ring, over almost all Europe except the British Isles and parts of the west and north.

Cretzschmar's Bunting *(E. caesia)*, rather like the Ortolan but with the throat orange, not yellow, in Greece and Asia Minor.

The Rustic Bunting *(E. rustica)*, rather like the Reed Bunting but with a white throat, in north-east Europe and northern Scandinavia.

The Lapland Bunting *(Calcarius lapponicus)*, which has a mainly black head, chestnut nape and black throat, with a range much like

◁ **Rock Sparrow** · *Petronia petronia* (p. 243) Above

◁ **Snow Finch** · *Montifringilla nivalis* (p. 244) Below

the Snow Bunting's, but excluding Iceland and Scotland (some winter in east England).

Brambling · *Fringilla montifringilla* L. (Illustration follows p. 219)

Family: Finches (Fringillidae)
Description: The ♂ in breeding plumage has the head, upper back and the greater part of the wings and tail black, the shoulders, throat and breast orange-red, and the belly and rump white. In autumn and winter the black is concealed by brownish and grey feather-edgings. The ♀ resembles the autumn-plumage ♂ but is duller. Juvenile plumage is like that of the ♀ but more brownish. L: 6", Wt: ⁴/₅ oz.

The song consists of a drawn-out "schrrreeng" and a few weak chirping notes. Single call-notes sound like "sweek", and a Linnet-like "gig-gig" is heard from birds in flight.

Distribution: Northern and north-eastern Europe, large regions of Asia above 50° N as far as the Kamchatka peninsula. It is for the most part migratory, wintering in mid- and southern Europe. Quite large numbers spend the winter in the British Isles.
Habitat: Open deciduous and mixed woods (especially birch forests) in the north; outside the breeding season fields, woods, parkland, even gardens. It is generally seen in flocks, often in association with other finches. The birds roost huddled close together on branches.

Breeding: The favourite site for the nest is in the fork of a branch, at no great height. It is a neatly rounded cup of grass, lichens and a little moss, with a lining of wool, hair and feathers. The four to seven eggs are bluish to brownish in ground colour, with smudgy blackish spots and brownish streaks. They are incubated by the ♀ alone, hatching after 12—14 days. The fledging period is about two weeks. The number of broods a pair rears in a season is uncertain.
Food: Chiefly insects in the breeding season, nestlings being fed entirely on these; also weed and tree seeds, especially beech-mast if available.

Nest and eggs of Carrion Crow · (p. 66) Above ▷

Nest and eggs of Golden Oriole · (p. 59) Below ▷

Chaffinch · *Fringilla coelebs* L.
(Illustration follows p. 223 and precedes p. 226, above)

Family: Finches (Fringillidae)
Description: In breeding plumage the ♂ has a blue-grey crown and nape, rather dark brown back, and greenish rump; its cheeks and underparts are vinous, tinged brown. There are two conspicuous white bars on the wing. In winter plumage the colours of the head and breast feathers are obscured by grey-brown or olive-brown feather-tips. The ♀ lacks the bright colours, although she has white wing-bars and outer tail feathers like the ♂. She is olive-brown above with a greenish rump, and somewhat paler below. Juveniles resemble the ♀.
L: 6″, Wt: 7/10 oz.

The Chaffinch's hard, shrill "pink" note is well-known. In some parts of its range it uses a rippling "trreeb" call, while elsewhere calls like "hweet" or "chit" are heard; the flight-note is a short "seep". The song is a pleasing, rapid, descending sequence which may be rendered as "chicheecheecheecheechoorichoo", although again the exact form varies as birds in each region have their own "dialect".

Distribution: Europe, with the exception of the extreme north and north-east, eastwards as far as 90° E, south-west Asia, north Africa. It is a partial migrant, wintering in mid- and southern Europe.
Habitat: All kinds of woodland, field hedges with trees, orchards, parks and gardens; outside the breeding season it occurs in flocks, often with other finches, on farmland and in stackyards.

Breeding: Already towards the end of winter the ♂♂ begin singing vigorously and fiercely defend their territories against others of their species. The nest may be in a bush or hedge, or quite high up in a tree; it is a deep, nicely rounded cup formed largely of moss, lichens and grass, with a lining of hair and wool, sometimes also feathers. The three to six eggs are buffish- or bluish-white, sparsely marked with deep purplish spots which have fuzzy reddish-brown edges. Incubation

◁ **Nest and eggs of Blackcap** · (p. 159) Above

◁ **Nest and eggs of Whinchat** · (p. 130) Below

238

is by the ♀ alone, the period being 12—13 days. The young leave the nest after about two weeks. Usually single-brooded in Britain, often double-brooded on the Continent.

Food: Weed seeds, buds, tree seeds; very largely insects and their larvae in the breeding season, the young being reared on these.

House Sparrow · *Passer domesticus* (L.)
(Illustration follows p. 227 and precedes p. 230)

Family: Weaverbirds (Ploceidae)
Description: The ♂ is brown above with dark streaks, its nape is reddish-brown and its crown grey. Its cheeks and underparts, apart from the black throat and breast, are pale grey. The black on the breast is obscured by grey feather-edgings after the summer moult. The ♀ is greyish-brown above with dark streaks, unstreaked greyish-white below. Young birds resemble the ♀. L: 6″, Wt: 1 oz.

The "song" of the ♂ is a rapid rhythmic "chilp-chilp". Frequently heard calls include the familiar "cheep" and when the bird is excited a chattering "teteteterrrrr".

Distribution: Europe, with the exception of Italy and Corsica, north Africa, the greater part of Asia up to 70° N, south to Ceylon and eastward as far as China, Arabia, Egypt. The species has been introduced into America and Australia. It is predominantly resident.
Habitat: It is very largely tied to areas of human habitation; in the south and west of its range it also occurs on farmland with hedgerows.

Breeding: The ♂ performs displays near the nest site, when it hops about with fluffed-up plumage and drooping wings and utters "chipping" calls. The ♀ encourages mating by crouching and wing-shivering, cheeping plaintively. Many nests are built in holes either in walls, under eaves, in trees, or nestboxes; others are in ivy or in open sites in trees or bushes, including the crowns of palm-trees in southern countries. The actual nest is an untidy domed structure of grass, lined

Nest and eggs of Tree Pipit · (p. 186) Above ▷

Nest and eggs of Whitethroat · (p. 162) Below ▷

with feathers. The three to six eggs are whitish with grey or brown spots or blotches. Incubation is by both sexes and lasts 11—14 days. The young fly after 13—18 days. Once the young are independent they move into ripening cornfields in large flocks. Two or three, occasionally four broods annually.

Food: The House Sparrow is omnivorous: it eats kitchen scraps, buds, seeds, grain, and many insects and larvae in the breeding season.

Italian Sparrow · *Passer (domesticus) italiae* (Vieill.)
(Illustration precedes p. 226)

Family: Weaverbirds (Ploceidae)
Description: Similar to the House Sparrow, the ♀♀ in particular being virtually indistinguishable. The ♂♂ are brighter and have chestnut crowns and whiter cheeks. Juveniles can hardly be told apart from young House Sparrows. L: 6″, Wt: 1 oz.

The "song" is the same as the House Sparrow's.

Distribution: Italy, hybridising with the House Sparrow in the north and the Spanish Sparrow *(Passer hispaniolensis)* in the south, Corsica.
Habitat, Breeding and *Food* are as in the House Sparrow.

Remarks: The Italian Sparrow is often regarded as a subspecies of the House Sparrow. Recent studies indicate that it originated through the interbreeding of House Sparrows and Spanish Sparrows.

Tree Sparrow · *Passer montanus* (L.) (Illustration follows p. 231)

Family: Weaverbirds (Ploceidae)
Description: ♂ and ♀ are brown above with dark streaks, greyish-white below. The crown is chestnut, the cheeks are whitish with a black spot on the ear-coverts and the throat is black. There is a pale indistinct collar round the neck. Juveniles closely resemble the adults. L: 5¹/₂″, Wt: ⁴/₅ oz.

◁ **Nest and eggs of Spotted Flycatcher** · (p. 175) Above

◁ **Nest and eggs of Red-backed Shrike** · (p. 198) Below

The calls are "tek-tek" and "cheek", also a chattering when agitated. The song is a highly variable twittering made up of these notes.

Distribution: All Europe except the north-east and southern Greece, in Asia extending from 65° N, and further northwards in places, right down to Indonesia, but excluding India. Predominantly resident, it wanders further than the House Sparrow. It too has been introduced into America and Australia.

Habitat: As for the House Sparrow, although it is more a bird of farmland, orchards and open country. In Britain it usually avoids close association with man.

Breeding: The Tree Sparrow breeds mainly in holes in trees, walls and roofs of barns, nestboxes, even in the ground in some countries. It quite often builds in the bases of old nests of birds like crows, but rarely chooses open sites among twigs except in the south. The nest is just like a House Sparrow's. A ♂ often owns several holes, making the beginnings of a nest in each, and vigorously defends them against other Tree Sparrows and other species. Sometimes tits or flycatchers trying to nest there are even killed by the ♂♂ Tree Sparrows. The three to seven eggs, smaller and rounder than House Sparrows', are whitish, usually densely flecked with reddish- or greyish-brown. Both sexes sit, incubation taking 11—13 days while the fledging period is 13—17 days. Double-brooded as a rule, sometimes treble-brooded.

Food: Similar to the House Sparrow's, but more weed seeds are taken; in the breeding season insects and larvae, especially caterpillars, form an important item; ladybirds (*Coccinella* and *Adalia*) and their larvae are eaten too.

Rock Sparrow · *Petronia petronia* (L.) (Illustration precedes p. 234)

Family: Weaverbirds (Ploceidae)

Description: Both sexes are rather like a hen House Sparrow, but they have a broad dark stripe over the eye, a cream-coloured stripe through it, white spots at the tip of the tail and a yellow spot on the throat, although this is sometimes hidden by the surrounding feathers. Juveniles resemble the parents. L: 5¹/₂″, Wt: 1¹/₄ oz.

Rock Sparrows utter a wheezy "weyee" call, and chatter like House

243

Sparrows when agitated. The song consists of a rhythmical, somewhat modulated repetition of the squeaky call note.

Distribution: South-western and southern Europe, north Africa, Asia Minor, various central- and east-Asian mountain ranges south of latitude 50°. It has become extinct north of the Alps since the start of the 20th century.
Habitat: Rocky country, ruined castles and old buildings.

Breeding: The nest is placed in rock-fissures, and in holes in trees, walls or in the ground; it resembles the House Sparrow's. Both sexes probably incubate the three to six eggs, the period being roughly 14 days. The young stay in the nest for just under three weeks.
Food: Similar to that of House and Tree Sparrows.

Snow Finch · *Montifringilla nivalis* (L.) (Illustration precedes p. 234)

Family: Weaverbirds (Ploceidae)
Description: ♂ and ♀ are greyish-brown above, with grey heads, white outer tail feathers and large white patches on the wings. The underside is off-white with a black patch on the throat. In breeding plumage, the bill of the ♂ is black, in winter plumage and in the ♀ it is pale. Juveniles resemble their parents but have no throat-patch, and their bills are orange-yellow. L: 7″, Wt: 1²/₅ oz.

The call notes sound like "zweek" and "tchip". The song is a hard twittering, often uttered on display-flights, during which the white tail feathers and largely white wings show up strikingly.

Distribution: The Alps, high mountain regions of southern Europe, south-west and central Asia. It is a resident, shifting down to lower altitudes in winter.
Habitat: High mountains above the tree limit right to the summer snow-line; it may be seen around mountain huts.

Breeding: The nest is placed far down in dark fissures in rocks or walls: an untidy structure of grass stems and roots with a lining of wool. The four or five pure white eggs are incubated by both sexes, hatching in 13—14 days. The fledging period is barely three weeks. Single- or double-brooded.
Food: Insects, spiders, weed seeds, also scraps.

TOPOGRAPHY OF A BIRD

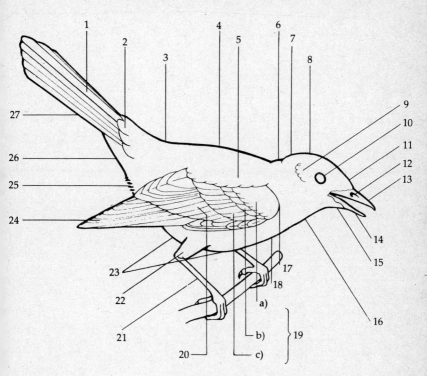

1 Tail feathers	12 Nostrils	20 Secondaries
2 Upper tail-coverts	13 Upper mandible	21 Tarsus
3 Rump	14 Lower mandible	22 Flank
4 Back	15 Chin	23 Belly
5 Scapulars	16 Throat	24 Primaries
6 Nape	17 Carpal joint	25 Vent
7 Back of head	18 Breast	26 Under tail-coverts
8 Crown	19 Wing-coverts	27 Outer tail feathers
9 Ear-coverts	a) lesser	
10 Eye	b) median	
11 Forehead	c) greater	

HEAD-MARKINGS

dark head
and pale stripe
above the eye

pale moustachial streak,
dark ear-coverts,
pale eye-ring

dark crown
and pale stripe
through the eye

TYPICAL IDENTIFICATION CHARACTERS

Wheatear with
characteristic
tail-pattern

House Martin from
above: white rump and
forked tail

TYPICAL POSTURES OF PASSERINE BIRDS

Thrush (Song Thrush)   Lark (Skylark)   Finch (Redpoll)

PRACTICAL BIRD CONSERVATION

Our bird life is being affected in an increasing variety of ways by man's activities. Old menaces such as excessive shooting, egg-collecting and illegal bird-catching have been reduced by legislation and enlightened opinion, but even greater dangers have arisen as a result of large-scale and rapid changes in land-use. One of the problems causing particular concern today is the effects which toxic pesticides may be having on bird populations, and possibly even on man himself. Measures to protect our bird population can only be effective if they are based on scientific research. We have to know where each species is found, how and why its numbers are changing, and what factors in both its winter- and summer-quarters are necessary for it to find food and breed successfully. Among the bodies concerned with such problems the British Trust for Ornithology has a unique countrywide network of members (mostly amateur) who put their bird-watching hobby to good use by gathering essential data on bird numbers, breeding success etc. Intensive research on birds is carried out at several universities, while particular problems or groups of birds are the subjects of investigation by the Nature Conservancy, the Ministry of Agriculture, the Wildfowl Trust and the Game Research Association. The Royal Society for the Protection of Birds is more concerned with maintaining reserves, and with education and law-enforcement, but is also conducting research on reserve management. These different bodies frequently co-operate in tackling problems of common interest. Some of them depend largely on their members' subscriptions to carry on their work, and everyone with an interest in birds can further the cause of conservation by joining at least one of these bodies. Protection problems affecting larger regions are in the sphere of the International Council for Bird Preservation, which consists of senior ornithologists representing each member country.

It is becoming increasingly clear that the best method of protecting birds is to conserve the natural environment or habitat in which they are adapted to live. Thus, where tracts of unspoilt countryside are fast disappearing the creation of reserves is particularly important; here again all nature lovers can help by supporting their local naturalists' trusts, which look after all aspects of natural history in their area.

Finally, here are a few practical ways in which the individual can help birds. The rooting-out of hedges and felling of old trees deprives many birds of nest sites, but some species will readily accept artificial sites. Hole-nesting birds can be encouraged by the provision of nestboxes, which should be fixed to tree-trunks at a height of at least 10 ft if they are in public places. Where cats or weasels are a menace the boxes may be fixed to hang freely from a wire. If boxes are exposed to the sun and rain, the entrance holes should face north-east. They are most likely to be used for nesting if erected in the previous autumn, so that birds can roost there during the winter. They should be cleaned out in late summer since old nest material harbours parasites, and if no inspection was made during the breeding season this would also show how many were occupied (empty ones may have been used by the ♂♂ for roosting). Boxes should not be put up near heavily-sprayed orchards, where what little insect-food the birds may find is likely to be contaminated by poisons. There is no space here to describe the many types of nestbox which can be made. The diameter of the entrance-hole is critical: for tits, Nuthatches, Redstarts and Pied Flycatchers it should measure $1^1/_4''$. To exclude House Sparrows it should be $1^1/_8''$; this still admits Tree Sparrows, but any further reduction excludes all but the smaller tits. Open-fronted boxes attract Robins and Spotted Flycatchers. Special asbestos-cement boxes are available for House Martins and Swallows, for use in places where they cannot find mud for nest-building.

No garden should lack a bird-bath; even a simple drinking place in the form of a shallow bowl 1 ft across is enough, provided that the rim is not slippery and that the water-level is maintained. Any risk of birds drowning in a deep vessel can be avoided by putting in stones to form an island. The provision of food helps birds through the winter. Peanuts and seeds like hemp, sunflower, millet, thistle, niger seed and poppy can be put out on trays or in hoppers. Cut-up raisins, oatmeal steeped in fat, and a mixture consisting of equal parts by weight of suet and wheat-bran provide nourishing food for insect-eaters. Tits, Nuthatches, treecreepers, woodpeckers, Starlings, Blackbirds, Robins, Wrens, Bullfinches and sparrows eagerly take this food, which is best hung up in shallow boxes. Proprietary mixtures of bird-food which attract many species may also be bought.

acrocephalus, from Gr. *ákros* pointed and Gr. *kephalé* the head

aegithalos, from Gr. *aigíthalos* the tit

agricola, Lat. the farmer

alauda, Lat. the lark

albicollis, from Lat. *albus* white and Lat. *collum* the neck

albus, a, um, Lat. white

alcedo, from Gr. *alkyón* the kingfisher

alpestris, e Lat. of the Alps

anthus, from Gr. *anthos* the blossom, flower; presumably from the bird's living on flowering meadows.

apiaster, from Lat. *apis* the bee

apus, from Gr. *ápous* without feet, not using the feet

arboreus, a, um Lat. of the tree

arundinaceus, from Lat. *arundo* the pipe, reed

arvensis, from Lat. *arvum* the arable or cornfield

ater, atra, atrum Lat. dark, black, without gloss

atricapilla, from Lat. *ater* black, and Lat. *capillus* the hair (of the head)

atrogularis, from Lat. *ater* black, and Lat. *gula* the throat

atthis Gr. Attic

aureolus, a, um Lat. golden

biarmicus, from Lat. *bis* doubly, and Lat. *armare* to equip or arm; refers to the two black moustachial stripes

bombycilla, from Gr. *bombyx* silk, and probably Lat. *culus* the tail

borealis, from Gr. *boréas* the north wind, northern

borin, Genoese name for a warbler

brachydactyla, from Gr. *brachydáctylos* short-fingered

caeruleus, a, um Lat. dark blue

caesius, a, um Lat. blue-grey, bluish-grey

calandra, from Gr. *kalándra* and *kálandros* a species of lark

calandrella, see *calandra*

calcarius, from Lat. *calcar* the spur

caligata, from Lat. *caligare* to be enveloped in darkness

calliope, from Gr. *kalliópé* the Muse of epic song or poetry

campester, -stris, -stre Lat. of the field

cannabinus, a, um from Gr. *kánnabis* hemp

cantillans, from Lat. *cantare* to sing, and Lat. *cantilena* the singing

canus, a, um Lat. grey, white

caprimulgus, Lat. the goatsucker or -milker

carduelis, from Lat. *carduus* the thistle

carpodacus, from Gr. *karpós* the fruit, and Gr. *dáknein* to bite

caryocatactes, from Gr. *karyokatáktes* the nutcracker

caudatus, from Lat. *cauda* the tail

cercotrichas, from Gr. *kérkos* the tail, and Gr. *trichás* a species of thrush

certhia, from Gr. *kérthios* the treecreeper

cervinus, a, um Lat. of the deer

cetti, cettia after the Italian naturalist of that name

chloris, from Gr. *chloros* of the colour of young corn; light green, greenish-yellow

cia Latinised onomatopoeia for the rock bunting's callnote.

cinclus, from Gr. *kinklos* a bird which often moves its tail up and down

cinerea, from Lat. *cinis* the ash, ash-grey

cinctus, from Lat. *cingere* to encircle, gird

cirlus Latinised onomatopoeia for the cirl bunting's song

cisticola, from Lat. *cistus* the rock-rose, and Lat. *colere* to dwell

citreola, from Gr. *kitréa* the lemon tree, lemon-yellow

citrinella, from Gr. *kitrinos* lemon-coloured

coccothraustes, from Gr. *kokkothraústes* the hawfinch

coelebs, from Lat. *caelebs* unmarried; ♂ and ♀ live apart outside the breeding season

collaris, from Lat. *collum* the neck

collurio, from Gr. *kollyríon* a bird of prey

collybita, from Gr. *kollybistés* the money-changer (after the song)

communis, Lat. ordinary, common

conspicillata, from Lat. *conspici* to be conspicuous

coracias, from Gr. *kórax*, the raven

corax, from Gr. *kórax* the raven

cornix, Lat. the crow

corone, from Gr. *koróne* the crow

corvus, Lat. the raven

cristatus, a, um Lat. having a crest

curruca, Latin bird-name of uncertain meaning (perhaps after the alarm call)

curviroster, -stra, -strum, from Lat. *curvus, a, um* bent or bowed, and Lat. *rostrum* the bill

cyanopica, from Gr. *kyáneos* dark blue, and Lat. *pica* the magpie

cyanurus, from Gr. *kyáneos* dark blue, and Gr. *ourá* the tail

cyanus, from Gr. *kyáneos* dark blue

daurica, perhaps derived from Gr. *taurikós* Tauric

delichon, anagram of Gr. *chelidon* the swallow

dendrocopos, from Gr. *dendrokopéo* to fell trees

domesticus, a, um Lat. belonging to the house, domestic

dryocopus, from Gr. *dryokópos* chopping wood

dumetorum, from Lat. *dumetum* wild hedge, thicket

emberiza latinised Saxon word for bunting ("ammer" as in Yellowhammer)

enucleator, from Lat. *enucleare* to crack or split kernels

epops Gr. the Hoopoe, named after its call

eremophila, from Gr. *eremophíles* loving solitude

erithacus, from Gr. *erithakos* the name of a bird

erythrinus, from Gr. *erythrós* red, dark red

europaeus Lat. European

excubitor Lat. the guard

familiaris Lat. domestic, social

ficédula, from Lat. *ficus* the fig; fig warbler

flammeus, a, um Lat. bright red, fiery red

flavirostris, from Lat. *flavus, a, um* golden yellow, and Lat. *rostrum* the bill

flavus, a, um Lat. golden yellow

fluviatilis Lat. living by the river

fringilla Lat. the finch, Gr. *phrygilos* a bird of unestablished identity

frugilegus, a, um Lat. gathering fruit, from Lat. *frux* the fruit and Lat. *legere* to gather

galactotes, probably from Gr. *galactoeidés* milk- or cream-coloured

galerida, from Lat. *galeritus, a, um* adorned with a feathered cap

garrulus, a, um, Lat. talkative, chattering

glandarius, from Lat. *glans* the acorn, *of* the acorn

graculus Lat. the jackdaw, latinised onomatopoeia for "crowing"

hippolais, from Gr. *hypolais* the singing warbler, and *hypolaléo* to gossip secretly, whisper.

hirundo Lat. the swallow

hispanicus, a, um Lat. Spanish

hispaniolensis, from Lat. *hispaniensis* living in Spain

hortensis, from Lat. *hortus* the garden

hortulana, from Lat. *hortus* the garden

hypoleuca, from Gr. *hypoleukos* white beneath, whitish

icterina, from Gr. *ikteros* jaundice; also a yellow bird, the sight of which was believed to cure jaundice

ignicapillus, from Lat. *ignis* the fire and Lat. *capillus* the hair of the head

iliacus, a, um Lat. belonging to Ilion, Trojan

infaustus, a, um Lat. bringing evil, unlucky

isabellina isabelline, creamy-buff

italia, ae Lat. Italian

juncidis, from Lat. *iuncus* the rush

jynx Gr. word for the Wryneck

lanius Lat. the butcher

lapponicus, a, um Lat. Lapplandish

leucoptera, from Gr. *leukópteros* white-winged

leucotos from Gr. *leukós* white

leucura, from Gr. *leúkuros* white-tailed

locustella, from Lat. *locusta* the grasshopper

loxia, from Gr. *loxós* bent sideways, crooked; and Gr. *loxias* nickname of Apollo, owing to the twisted, obscure oracles he uttered.

lugubris Lat. of mourning

lullula Latinised onomatopoeia for the woodlark's song

luscinia Lat. the Nightingale

luscinioides, from Lat. *luscinia* the Nightingale and Gr. ending *-eides* meaning of the same sort

major Lat. greater

martius, a, um Lat. warlike, belonging to Mars

medius, a, um Lat. the middle one

megarhynchos, from Gr. *mégas* large, and Gr. *rhynchos* the bill

melanocephala, from Gr. *mélas* black, and Gr. *kephalé* the head

melanocorypha, from Gr. *mélas* black, and Gr. *koryphé* the top, crown *melanopogon*, from Gr. *mélas* black, and Gr. *pógon* beard

melba, latinised German dialect-word meaning mealy

mérops Gr. the bee-eater

merula Lat. the Blackbird

minor Lat. the lesser

modularis, from Lat. *modulari* to sing in time, melodiously

monedula Lat. the Jackdaw

montanus, a, um living on the mountains

monticola, Lat. the inhabitant of the mountains

montifringilla, from Lat. *mons* the mountain, and Lat. *fringilla* the finch

motacilla, from Lat. *motare* and *movere* to move, and probably Lat. *culus* the tail

muraria, from Lat. *murus* the wall

muscicapa, from Lat. *musca* the fly, and Lat. *capere* to catch

naevius, a, um from Lat. *naevus* the birthmark, spotted

nisorius, a, um latinisation for sparrow hawk-like, from Lat. *Nisus*, king of Megara, who was changed into a Sparrow Hawk

nivalis Lat. of snow, snow-white

nubicus, from Lat. *nubes* the cloud

nucifraga, from Lat. *nux* the nut, and Lat. *frangere* to break

ochruros from Gr. *ochrós* pale yellow, and Gr. *ourá* the tail

oenanthe, from Gr. *oinánthe* the fruiting bud of the vine. Name of the Wheatear, perhaps because it breeds in vineyards

olivetorum, from Lat. *olivetum* the olive grove

oriolus, from Lat. *aureolus*, diminutive of *aureus* golden

pallidus, a, um Lat. pale

paludicola, from Lat. *palus* the swamp and Lat. *colere* to dwell, inhabit

palustris, Lat. swampy, swamp-inhabiting

panurus, from Gr. *pan* all, the whole, and Gr. *ourá* the tail, referring in the Bearded Tit to its long tail

parus Lat. the tit

parvus, a, um Lat. small

passer Lat. the sparrow

pendulinus, from Lat. *pendulus, a, um* hanging, referring to the Penduline Tit's suspended nest

perisoreus, presumably from Gr. *peri* around, and Lat. *risor* the laugher

petronia, from Gr. *pétros* the stone or rock

philomelos, from Gr. *philos* friend, and Gr. *mélos* song, melody

phoenicurus, from Gr. *phoiník-ouros* the redstart

phylloscopus, from Gr. *phyllon* the leaf, and Gr. *skopéo* to examine, spy into

pica Lat. the Magpie

picoides, from Lat. *picus* the woodpecker, and Gr. ending -*eides* meaning of the same sort

picus Lat. the woodpecker

pilaris, from Lat. *pilus* the hair, the hairbrush

pinicola, from Lat. *pinus* the pine, and Lat. *colere* to dwell, inhabit

plectrophenax, from Gr. *plek-tron* the spur, and Gr. *phénax* the deceiver

pleschanka Russian bird-name

polyglotta, from Gr. *polys* many, and Gr. *glóssa* the tongue, language

pratensis Lat. of meadows

prunella probably from Lat.

prunum the plum, concerning the grey plumage of the Dunnock's breast

pusillus, a, um Lat. very small

pyrrhocorax from Gr. *pyrrhós* fiery red, reddish, and Gr. *kórax* the raven

pyrrhula, from Gr. *pyrrhós* fiery red, concerning the bird's breast

pytyopsittacus, from Gr. *pitys* pine, fir, and Gr. *psittakos* parrot

regulus Lat. little king

remiz Polish the Penduline Tit

riparius, a, um Lat. nesting in banks

rubecula, from Lat. *ruber* red

rubetra, from Lat. *ruber* red

rufescens from Lat. *rufus* rufous

ruficollis, from Lat. *rufus, a, um* rufous, and Lat. *collum* the neck

rupestris, from Lat. *rupes* the rock

rusticus, a, um Lat. rural

sardus, a, um Lat. Sardinian

saxatilis Lat. dwelling among the rocks

saxicola, from Lat. *saxum* the rock, Lat. *colere* to dwell

schoeniclus, from Gr. *schoínos* the reed

schoenobaenus, from Gr. *schoínos* the reed, and Gr. *baíno* to go, stride

scirpaceus, from Lat. *scirpus* the reed

semitorquata, from Lat. *semi* half, and Lat. *torquatus, a, um* wearing a necklace

senator Lat. the senator, after the purple-striped toga worn by Roman senators

serinus Latinised onomatopoeia for the serin's call-note

sibilatrix, from Lat. *sibilare* to whistle

sitta, from Gr. *sítte* a species of nuthatch, also onomatopoeic

solitarius, a, um Lat. solitary, unsociable

spinoletta, from Lat. *spina* the thorn

spinus, from Lat. *spina* thorn, referring to the Siskin's pointed bill, and Gr. *spínos* a small bird, called after its squeaky voice (Siskin)

striatus Lat. finely streaked

sturnus Lat. the Starling

svecicus, a, um Lat. Swedish

sylvia, origin unknown, perhaps from Lat. *silva* the wood, shrubbery

syriacus, from Gr. *syriakós* Syrian

tarsiger, origin uncertain

theklae, from Gr. *Thekla*, woman's name

tichodroma, from Gr. *teichos*, the wall, and Gr. *dromeús*, the runner

torquatus, a, um, from Lat., wearing a necklace

torquilla, from Lat. *torquere*, to bend, twist

tridactylus, from Gr. *tridáktylos*, three-fingered

trivialis, from Lat., common

trochiloides, from Gr. *trochilos* a kind of small bird, and Gr. ending *-eides* meaning of the same sort

trochilus, from Gr. *trochilos*, a kind of small bird

troglodytes, from Gr., dwelling in caves, name of the Wren

turdus, Lat., the thrush

undatus, a, um, from Lat. *undare*, to undulate, lift

upupa, Lat., the Hoopoe

urbicus, a, um, Lat. urban

viridis, Lat., green

viscivorus, from Lat. *viscum*, the mistletoe, and Lat. *vorare*, to devour

vulgaris, Lat., common

yeltoniensis, of the Yelton Sea, east of the Volga

ABBREVIATIONS OF AUTHORS' NAMES

Bechst. = Johann Matthaeus Bechstein (1757–1822)
Bodd.   = Pieter Boddaert (1730–1796)
Brehm = Christian Ludwig Brehm (1787–1864)
Gmel.   = Joannes Friedrich Gmelin (1748–1804)
Herm.   = Johann (also Jean) Hermann (1738–1800)
Lath.   = John Latham (1740–1837)
L.   = Carolus Linnaeus; later: Carl von Linné (1707–1778)
Pall.   = Peter Simon Pallas (1741–1811)
Savi   = Paola Savi (1798–1871)
Tunst. = Marmaduke Tunstall (1743–1790)
Vieill. = Louis Jean Pierre Vieillot (1748–1828)

INDEX

Figures in **bold** refer to illustrations

Acrocephalus agricola 155
– arundinaceus 147, **148**
– dumetorum 155
– melanopogon 155
– paludicola 155
– palustris 151, **156**
– schoenobaenus 154, **157**
– scirpaceus **149**, 150, **152**, **153**
Aegithalos caudatus 98, **100**
Alauda arvensis 51, **52**, **53**
Alcedo atthis **21**, 23, **24**, **25**
Alpine Accentor 183
Anthus campestris 186
– cervinus 186
– gustavi 186
– pratensis **181**, 183
– richardi 186
– spinoletta 186
– trivialis 186, **240**
Apus apus 19, **20**
– melba **17**, 18
– pallidus 19

Bee-eater 26, **28**
Blackbird 122, **124**
Blackcap 159, **160**, **237**
Bluetail, Red-flanked 138
Bluethroat 139, **140**, **141**
Bombycilla garrulus **188**, 191
Brambling **220**, **221**, 235
Bullfinch **205**, 218
Bunting, Black-headed 234
　Cirl **212**, 223
　Corn **213**, 227
　Cretzschmar's 234
　Lapland 234
　Little **217**, 231
　Ortolan 234
　Reed **213**, 226
　Rock **216**, 230
　Rustic 234
　Snow **217**, 231
　Yellow-breasted 234
Bush Chat, Rufous 146

Calandrella brachydactyla 54
– rufescens 54

Calcarius lapponicus 234
Caprimulgus europaeus **21**, 22
– ruficollis 22
Carduelis cannabina **201**, 215
– carduelis **197**, 206
– chloris **196**, 203
– citrinella **200**, 211
– flammea **200**, 210
– flavirostris **201**, 214
– spinus **197**, 207
Carpodacus erythrinus 219
Cercotrichas galactotes 146
Certhia brachydactyla 107
– familiaris 106, **109**
Cettia cetti 155
Chaffinch **224**, **225**, 238
Chiffchaff **168**, 170
Chough 74
　Alpine 71, **72**
Cinclus cinclus 110, **113**
Cisticola juncidis 155
Coccothraustes
　coccothraustes **196**, 202
Coracias garrulus **29**, 30
Corvus corax 62, **64**
– corone cornix 67, **68**
– corone corone **65**, 66, **236**
– frugilegus **69**, 70
– monedula 74, **76**
Crossbill **208**, 219
　Parrot 222
　Two-barred 222
Crow, Carrion **65**, 66
　Hooded 67, **68**
Cyanopica cyanus 78

Delichon urbica 55, **56**
Dendrocopus leucotos 43
– major **4**, 43, **44**
– medius 39, **40**
– minor **41**, 42
– syriacus 43
Dipper 110, **113**
Dryocopus martius **45**, 46
Dunnock **180**, 182

Emberiza aureola 234
– caesia 234
– calandra **213**, 227
– cia **216**, 230
– cirlus **212**, 223
– citrinella **209**, 222
– hortulana 234
– melanocephala 234
– pusilla **217**, 231
– rustica 234
– schoeniclus **213**, 226
Eremophila alpestris **49**, 50
Erithacus rubecula **136**, **137**, 138

Ficedula albicollis 179
– hypoleuca **177**, 178
– parva 179
– semitorquata 179
Fieldfare 114, **117**
Finch, Citril **200**, 211
　Snow **233**, 244
Firecrest 175
Flycatcher, Collared 179
　Pied **177**, 178
　Red-breasted 179
　Spotted 175, **176**, **241**
Fringilla coelebs **224**, **225**, 238
– montifringilla **220**, **221**, 235

Galerida cristata 47, **48**
– theklae 50
Garrulus glandarius 79, **80**
Goatsucker **21**, 22
Goldcrest **173**, 174
Goldfinch **197**, 206
Great Grey Shrike **189**, 194
Greenfinch **196**, 203
Grosbeak, Pine 219
　Scarlet 219

Hawfinch **196**, 202
Hippolais caligata 159
– icterina 155, **156**
– olivetorum 159
– pallida 158
– polyglotta 158

Hirundo daurica 59
– rupestris 59
– rustica **57**, 58
Hoopoe 31, **32**

Jackdaw 74, **76**
Jay 79, **80**
Siberian 79, **80**
Jynx torquilla **33**, 34

Kingfisher **21**, 23, **24**, **25**

Lanius collurio **192**, 198, **241**
– excubitor **189**, 194
– minor 199
– nubicus 199
– senator **189**, 195
Lark, Black 54
Calandra 54
Crested 47, **48**
Lesser Short-toed 54
Shore **49**, 50
Short-toed 54
Sky 51, **52**, **53**, **240**
Thekla 50
White-winged 54
Wood **49**, 50
Linnet **201**, 215
Locustella fluviatilis 147
– luscinioides **145**, 146
– naevia 147
Loxia curvirostra **208**, 219
– leucoptera 222
– pytyopsittacus 222
Lullula arborea **49**, 50
Luscinia calliope 142
– luscinia 143, **144**
– megarhynchos 143, **144**
– svecica 139, **140**, **141**

Magpie 75, **77**
Azure-winged 78
Martin, Crag 59
House 55, **56**
Sand 55, **56**
Melanocorypha calandra 54
– leucoptera 54
– yeltoniensis 54
Merops apiaster 26, **28**
Monticola saxatilis 134
– solitarius 131, **132**

Montifringilla nivalis **233**, 244
Motacilla alba **181**, 186
– cinerea **184**, 187
– citreola 191
– flava **185**, 190
Muscicapa striata 175, **176**, **241**

Nightingale 143, **144**
Thrush 143, **144**
Nightjar **21**, 22
Red-necked 22
Nucifraga caryocatactes **81**, 82
Nutcracker **81**, 82
Nuthatch 102, **105**
Corsican 103
Rock 103

Oenanthe hispanica 127
– isabellina 127
– leucura 123, **124**
– oenanthe **125**, 126
– pleschanka 127
Oriole, Golden 59, **60**, **236**
Oriolus oriolus 59, **60**, **236**
Ouzel, Ring 119, **121**

Panurus biarmicus 99, **104**
Parus ater 91, **96**
– caeruleus, **89**, 90, **92**
– cinctus 90
– cristatus 94, **96**
– cyanus 91
– lugubris 90
– major 83, **84**, **85**, **88**
– montanus 90
– palustris 87, **88**, **93**
Passer domesticus **228**, **229**, 239
– (domesticus) italiae **225**, 242
– hispaniolensis 242
– montanus **232**, 242
Perisoreus infaustus 79, **80**
Petronia petronia **233**, 243
Phoenicurus ochruros **132**, 134
– phoenicurus **133**, 135
Phylloscopus bonelli 167, **168**
– borealis 174

– collybita **168**, 170
– sibilatrix 171, **172**
– trochiloides 174
– trochilus **169**, 170
Pica pica 75, **77**
Picoides tridactylus 43
Picus canus **37**, 38
– viridis 35, **36**
Pinicola enucleator 219
Pipit, Meadow **181**, 183
Petchora 186
Red-throated 186
Richard's 186
Rock 186
Tawny 186
Tree 186, **240**
Water 186
Plectrophenax nivalis **217**, 231
Prunella collaris 183
– modularis **180**, 182
Pyrrhocorax graculus 71, **72**
– pyrrhocorax 74
Pyrrhula pyrrhula **205**, 218

Raven 62, **64**
Redpoll **200**, 210
Redstart **133**, 135
Black **132**, 134
Redwing **121**, 122
Regulus ignicapillus 175
– regulus **173**, 174
Remiz pendulinus 95, **97**
Riparia riparia 55, **56**
Robin **136**, **137**, 138
Roller **29**, 30
Rook **69**, 70
Rubythroat, Siberian 142

Saxicola rubetra **129**, 130, **237**
– torquata 127, **128**
Serin **204**, 215
Serinus serinus **204**, 215
Shore Lark **49**, 50
Shrike, Great Grey **189**, 194
Lesser Grey 199
Masked 199
Red-backed **192**, 198, **241**
Woodchat **189**, 195
Siskin **197**, 207

Sitta europaea 102, **105**
− neumayer 103
− whiteheadi 103
Skylark 51, **52, 53**
Sparrow, Hedge
 (see Dunnock)
 House **228, 229,** 239
 Italian **225,** 242
 Rock **233,** 243
 Spanish 242
 Tree **232,** 242
Starling **193,** 199
 Rose-coloured 202
 Spotless 202
Stonechat 127, **128**
Sturnus roseus 202
− unicolor 202
− vulgaris **193,** 199
Swallow **57,** 58
 Red-rumped 59
Swift 19, **20**
 Alpine 18
 Pallid 19
Sylvia atricapilla 159, **160,**
 237
− borin **165,** 166
− cantillans 167
− communis 162, **164, 240**
− conspicillata 167
− curruca 163, **164**
− hortensis 167
− melanocephala 167
− nisoria **161,** 162
− rüppelli 167
− sarda 167
− undata 167

Tarsiger cyanurus 138
Thrush, Black-throated 123
 Blue Rock 131, **132**
 Mistle 111, **116**
 Rock 134
 Song 115, **120**
Tichodroma muraria 103,
 108

Tit, Azure 91
 Bearded 99, **104**
 Blue **89,** 90, **92**
 Coal 91, **96**
 Crested 94, **96**
 Great 83, **84, 85, 88**
 Long-tailed 98, **100**
 Marsh 87, **88, 93**
 Penduline 95, **97**
 Siberian 90
 Sombre 90
 Willow 90
Treecreeper 106, **109**
 Short-toed 107
Troglodytes troglodytes 107,
 112
Turdus atrogularis 123
− iliacus **121,** 122
− merula 122, **124**
− philomelos 115, **120**
− pilaris 114, **117**
− torquatus 119, **121**
− viscivorus 111, **116**
Twite **201,** 214

Upupa epops 31, **32**

Wagtail, Citrine 191
 Grey **184,** 187
 Pied **181,** 186
 White 186
 Yellow **185,** 190
Wallcreeper 103, **108**
Warbler, Aquatic 155
 Arctic 174
 Barred **161,** 162
 Blyth's Reed 155
 Bonelli's 167, **168**
 Booted 159
 Cetti's 155
 Dartford 167
 Fan-tailed 155
 Garden **165,** 166
 Grasshopper 147
 Great Reed 147, **148**

 Greenish 174
 Icterine 155, 156
 Marmora's 167
 Marsh 151, **156**
 Melodious 158
 Moustached 155
 Olivaceous 158
 Olive-tree 159
 Orphean 167
 Paddyfield 155
 Reed **149,** 150, **152, 153**
 River 147
 Rüppell's 167
 Sardinian 167
 Savi's **145,** 146
 Sedge 154, **157**
 Spectacled 167
 Subalpine 167
 Willow **169,** 170
 Wood 171, **172**
Waxwing **188,** 191
Wheatear **125,** 126
 Black 123, **124**
 Black-eared 127
 Isabelline 127
 Pied 127
Whinchat **129,** 130, **237**
Whitethroat 162, **164, 240**
 Lesser 163, **164**
Willow Tit 90
Willow Warbler **169,** 170
Woodpecker, Black **45,** 46
 Great Spotted 43, **44**
 Green 35, **36**
 Grey-headed **37,** 38
 Lesser Spotted **41,** 42
 Middle Spotted 39, **40**
 Syrian 43
 Three-toed 43
 White-backed 43
Wryneck **33,** 34
Wren 107, **112**

Yellowhammer **209,** 222

LIST OF PHOTOGRAPHERS

(a. = above, b. = below)

A. Aichhorn, Austria: 108, 121 a., 168 a., 197 b., 200 a., 217 b., 233 b., 236 b. – W. A. Bajohr, Germany: 213 a. – F. Bretzendorfer, Germany: 17 – A. Christiansen, Denmark: 56 b., 68, 76, 140, 144 b., 152/153, 177, 180, 205, 209, 217 a. – K. Conrads, Germany: 36, 49 a. – E. Erdmann, Germany: 49 b., 88 a., 116, 156 a., 156 b., 168 b., 181 b., 196 b., 197 a., 201 a., 201 b. – H. Fischer, Germany: 45 – H. Hinz, Switzerland: 100/101 – E. Hosking, England: 77, 213 b. – Dr. C. König, Germany: 69, 72/73, 124 b., 132 a., 236 a., 237 b., 241 b. – E. Kuch, Germany: 21 b. – H. Landvogt, Germany: 24, 40, 65 b., 96 b., 105, 192 – H. Laßwitz, Germany: 4, 25, 44, 60, 61, 89, 132 b., 181 a., 193 – A. Limbrunner, Germany: 33 – Dr. H. Löhrl, Germany: 237 a. – Ilse Makatsch, Germany: 56 a. – S. O. Martin, Germany: 225 a., 225 b. – H. Olsson, Sweden: 84, 85, 88 b., 92, 93, 117, 124 a., 129, 136/137, 157, 165, 169, 172, 185, 224, 228 – G. Quedens, Germany: 125, 164 b. – O. Schmid, Sweden: 149, 208 – H. Schrempp, Germany: 65 a., 96 a., 121 b., 233 a. – H. Schünemann, Germany: 184 – D. Schuphan, Germany: 212, 216 – K. Schwammberger, Germany: 20, 21 a., 37, 81, 188, 189 a., 200 b., 229, 232, 240 b., 241 a. – K.-H. Schwammberger, Germany: 220/221 – L. Schwarz, Germany: 113 – R. Simon, Germany: 128, 240 a. – D. Skruzny, Germany: 120, 189 b. – K. Söding, Germany: 196 a. – P. O. Swanberg, Sweden: 41, 160 – M. Temme, Germany: 104 – A. Thielemann, Germany: 164 a. – W. Tilgner, Switzerland: 80 b. – H. Tomanek, Germany: 57 – J. Waskala, Germany: 80 a. – K. Weber, Switzerland: 28, 29, 109 – F. Wenzel, Denmark: 64, 173 – W. Wissenbach, Germany: 133, 176 – W. Zimmermann, Germany: 48 – D. Zingel, Germany: 32, 52/53, 97, 112, 141, 144 a., 145, 148, 161, 204